THE INTERSECTION BETWEEN

Faith and Forgiveness

A HEALING JOURNEY

Dr. Marie Brown Mercadel

ISBN: 978-1-962402-21-7

Cover photography by: Dave Frank, Portrait Creations

Published by
Fideli Publishing, Inc.

www.FideliPublishing.com

What people are saying about *Intersection* ...

Dr. Marie does it again—an absolute home run!

"This second book took me by surprise with its depth and insight—far more than I anticipated. As a man, I didn't expect to connect so deeply with the content, but I found myself both in tears and cheering for the courageous journey laid bare on these pages. Her vulnerability and honesty are nothing short of remarkable. I was captivated from start to finish and felt like I came to know her on an even deeper level. This book is not only inspirational, but also profoundly thought-provoking."

— Harold Tuck, MBA

As someone who has endured my own childhood trauma, reading Dr. Marie's story was both validating and deeply moving. Her willingness to confront unthinkable pain with honesty and grace resonated with my own journey of post-traumatic growth. I saw pieces of myself in her struggles, her courage, and most of all, in her choice to forgive. This book reminded me that healing isn't about forgetting—it's about reclaiming your life with purpose and compassion. Dr. Marie's story gave language to emotions I've long carried, and it reminded me that we are never alone in the fight to become whole again.

— Isaac Ford Jr., MSW
MGySgt. USMC, Retired, and Author of *Up from the Bottom*

Dr. Marie's latest book is nothing short of a masterpiece. The Intersection Between Faith and Forgiveness is a soul-stirring journey of courage, healing, and divine grace. Her transparency in sharing the darkest valleys of her life—and the unwavering faith that carried her through—is both humbling and inspiring. This book reminds us that true healing begins where faith meets forgiveness, and that God can take even our deepest wounds and turn them into powerful testimonies. If you've ever struggled to let go of pain, or wondered if healing was possible for you, this book will breathe life into your spirit. I am so grateful for Dr. Marie's obedience to tell her story—because in doing so, she gives others permission to heal."

— Tamera Trotter, MA
Host, *Win Over Depression* Podcast, Speaker, Mentor, Certified Trainer

Dedication

To my late beloved sisters, **Gwen, Joyce, and Mary**, whose strength, love, and wisdom have shaped me in more ways than I can count. Your unwavering support and presence were a beacon of hope in my journey.

To the **beautiful women of the Brown family**—especially my nieces, a lineage of resilience, grace, and courage—this book is for you. May our stories continue to inspire, heal, and uplift generations to come.

To **Bryce, Brooklyn, and Chantell**, thank you for the light you bring into my world. Your love, laughter, and warmth remind me daily of the beauty in life's journey.

To my brother **Arthur, Jr.,** thank you for being a steady source of support in my life. You are one of the good guys.

And to **Alvin**—30 years in, through the fires and the storms, I can still see the rainbows and the beauty in our love. Thank you for standing beside me, for carrying me, for your strength, and for always allowing me to be who I am.

Table of Contents

Forward with Fortitude

Note to Readers

This book contains discussions of sensitive topics, including sexual harm, domestic violence, and death. These experiences are deeply personal and, for many, may bring up painful memories or emotions. If you have encountered similar trauma in your own life, please know that you are not alone.

My hope in sharing my story is not to retraumatize you, but to bring awareness, understanding, and hope. If at any point this book becomes overwhelming, please give yourself the grace to step away and return when you feel ready. Your well-being matters. Above all, know that healing is possible, and you are never alone on this journey.

As you read, I encourage you to engage with this content in a way that honors your emotional well-being. Healing is a personal journey, and there is no right or wrong way to navigate it.

You may also wish to consider the following suggestions:

- Speak to someone in your circle of support to discuss your thoughts.

- Skip the sections that cause harmful memories.

- Keep a journal describing the passages that were upsetting. You might think about speaking to a therapist to discuss strategies for healing.

- Read the book at a time that does not interfere with your ability to sleep or work.

- If you need resources, please call the RAINN National Sexual Assault Telephone Hotline at 800-656-HOPE.

- If suicidal thoughts occur, please call the National Suicide Prevention Lifeline at 800-873-TALK.

Also by the Author

In her first book, *Getting to My Enough*, Dr. Marie Brown Mercadel shares her extraordinary journey of perseverance through childhood sexual trauma, the loss of a baby as a teenager, and her unwavering determination to reach a place of healing and self-worth. With raw honesty and vivid detail, she recounts her struggles with self-doubt, fear, and shame—emotions that shaped much of her adult life.

Through acts of forgiveness and the embrace of self-love, she found the strength to reclaim her narrative and chart a new path forward. *Getting to My Enough* is more than a memoir; it is a testament to resilience, inner peace, and the power of transformation. Her story serves as both an inspiration and a call to action for women facing similar challenges, proving that even in the face of deep pain, healing and triumph are possible.

Author's Message

This book reflects the transformative power of forgiveness, grace, and faith. It chronicles my journey—one that began in deep pain but ultimately led me to healing, self-acceptance, and peace. Forgiveness was not an easy choice, but it became my path to freedom, releasing me from the burden of resentment that had held me captive for so long.

To truly forgive, I had to give myself grace—to allow space for grief, anger, questioning, and struggle. I had to unlearn the belief that strength meant suppressing my emotions. Instead, I discovered that true strength lies in vulnerability, in giving myself permission to feel deeply and still choosing to move forward. Grace taught me that healing is not a straight path, that setbacks are not failures, and that I am deserving of compassion—even from myself.

Through it all, my faith became my foundation. In moments of despair, faith reminded me that I was never alone. When the pain felt unbearable, it was my faith that carried me through. I leaned into God's love, trusting that even in my brokenness, I remained whole in His eyes. My faith gave me the courage to keep going, to believe in something greater than my pain, and to find purpose in my story.

I share my journey not just for myself, but for others who have walked a similar path. For those who have struggled with shame, with forgiveness, or with feeling unworthy—I see you. I pray that my story offers you hope and that it reminds you healing is possible.

This book is my offering, my truth, and my testimony. May it inspire you to embark on your own healing, to extend grace to yourself, to hold onto faith, and to know—without a doubt—that you are enough.

Foreword

As a childhood trauma survivor who has been a victim of neglect and emotional abuse, I often find it hard to forgive those who have contributed to my past suffering and anguish. However, this book sheds light on the understanding that "forgiveness involves releasing the hold that past hurt has on one's present life."

Written by Dr. Marie, whose life embodies the principles she champions, this book shares her journey of strength and resilience—not just in overcoming her own trials, but in guiding others toward healing.

Her story is a testament that it is possible to rise from pain and turn it into a source of strength and transformation.

She has become a beacon of hope for those struggling to break free from the weight of their past. Dr. Marie has not only transformed her own life but has made it her mission to empower others. She has turned her personal wounds into a source of strength, offering a blueprint that is grounded in the belief that each of us has the power to reclaim our narrative.

Trauma, in all its forms, can leave us feeling isolated, lost, and powerless. Dr. Marie shows us that it is possible to heal and move forward with hope and forgiveness in our hearts, even when it seems impossible. As you read, I hope you find the courage to begin your own journey and discover the transformative strength that lies within you. May you, too, embrace the path to forgiveness, find the courage to heal, and harness the power to become the change you wish to see in the world.

Dr. Shanee Morgan
Author, *Shaken Yet Here I Stand*
Social Change Agent, Keynote Speaker, Coach

A Call to Compassion

"Your truth challenges shame.
Your voice dismantles stigma.
Healing out loud is how we shift
the narrative of trauma."

— Dr. Marie Brown Mercadel

CHAPTER I

Digging Deep

> *Be kind and compassionate to one another, forgiving each other, just as in Christ God forgave you.*
>
> ~ Ephesians 4:32

Each morning, I called my older sister, Mary. It had become more than a habit; it was my lifeline to her, a way of reassuring myself that she was doing okay. Her diagnosis of chronic obstructive pulmonary disease (COPD) and congestive heart failure weighed heavily on both of us. Our conversations were often mundane, revolving around neighborhood gossip or her constant curiosity about what I was planning to cook for dinner. But one morning, Mary's voice carried a tension that cut through the usual pleasantries. "I know you don't want to hear this," she began hesitantly, "but your brother is in the hospital. They found a tumor on his brain."

She didn't need to say his name. I knew she was talking about Edward, the oldest of my three brothers. His shadow had loomed large over my childhood, a reminder of pain and betrayal. When I was between the ages of seven and ten, he had violated my trust in the most unforgivable ways by sexually assaulting me on numerous occasions.

Mary understood my reluctance to hear about him, but this news was something she couldn't withhold. For years, I had lived with the consequences of what he'd done, compartmentalizing the memories to survive. Despite my usual resolve to block Edward from my mind, I found myself asking for more details about his condition, driven by something I couldn't quite put into words. Against all logic, I listened intently, trying to understand what happened.

Mary explained that Edward had collapsed in the parking lot of a local convenience store and was transported by ambulance to Onslow Memorial Hospital in Jacksonville, North Carolina. He was treated for bruises from his fall and sent home, but the next morning, his friends found him at home, on the floor, unable to move. He was taken back to the hospital and a CT scan revealed a mass in his frontal lobe. Due to the hospital's limited resources, he was transferred an hour away to East Carolina University Hospital in Greenville, North Carolina, for specialized care. As she recounted the events, I felt a tangle of emotions—sympathy, fear, and confusion—but one feeling was undeniable: I needed to go see him.

I wasn't entirely sure why I felt compelled to visit Edward in the hospital. Perhaps it was the mantle I had assumed as the family matriarch after my parents, Arthur Sr., and Ernestine, passed away, followed by the deaths of my sisters Gwen and Beverly. Although I am the youngest girl of seven children, the responsibility of keeping together the remaining pieces of our fractured family often fell to me. Or perhaps it was something deeper—an unspoken need for closure.

Yet beyond my personal motivations, the stark reality was that Edward had no one else. My sister Mary, incapacitated by her illness, rarely left home except for medical appointments and was physically incapable of visiting Edward in the hospital. My brother Arthur Jr., while emotionally supportive of me, had been estranged from Edward for years due to his actions against me as a child and declined to take part in his care—and I understood his position.

I also chose not to expose my female nieces to him, even in his final days, as their safety and well-being were not something I was willing to compromise. In the end, the painful truth was clear: despite being the victim of his abuse, I was his only option. So, I asked my husband, Alvin, to accompany me to the hospital. Without hesitation, he packed a bag, his quiet support reminding me that I didn't have to face this alone.

The four-hour drive from Charlotte to Greenville was heavy with silence. I could feel Alvin's occasional glances, likely wondering how I would respond when I finally stood face to face with Edward. I stared out the window, my thoughts racing back to moments I had buried long ago. Edward's laughter when we were children, the protective brother I had looked up to before everything changed. And then, the memories I wished I could erase—the betrayal, the pain, and the worry. Alvin occasionally reached over to squeeze my hand, his silent reassurance anchoring me. Still, I wondered what I was doing. What could I possibly say to a man who had stolen my innocence?

When we arrived at East Carolina University Hospital, I felt a wave of dread. I closed my eyes and murmured a prayer, asking God for strength and an open heart. Stepping out of the car, I felt the immense weight of what awaited me, pressing down like an unshakable burden. This wasn't just a hospital visit—it was the intersection of my past trauma and the present reality of my brother's illness. I wondered if I was ready for this confrontation.

Could I look Edward in the eyes and not see the man who violated the trust of a blameless child? My mind raced back to the last time I had crossed paths with him a couple of years prior, the day he arrived uninvited to a Mother's Day dinner at my childhood home. It was upsetting, and I had promised myself that I would never let him hold any power over me again. And yet, standing at the entrance of the hospital, the anxiety swirling in my chest, it was clear that he still did. I tried to remind myself why I had come—to seek closure, to find peace, to forgive if I could.

The building loomed before us, cold and imposing, its gray exterior mirroring the heaviness in my chest. The scent of disinfectants and the soft hum of classical music did little to ease my rising anxiety as we entered the doors. We stopped at the visitor's station, provided our information, and had our photographs taken for the temporary badges. The attendant gave us directions to the oncology ward and as we approached my steps grew slower and heavier. In the background, the hospital was a blur of activity—nurses rushing past, doctors engrossed in charts, families speaking in hushed tones.

It all felt distant, like I was watching a scene unfold through a fogged window. The sharp scent of antiseptic stung my nose, and the hum of the HVAC system seemed deafening against the silence of my thoughts. My heart pounded as memories surfaced with startling clarity—moments of blame, shame, and anger. I had convinced myself that I had moved on, but now, as I moved closer to Edward's room, I realized how much of the past I still carried with me.

The door to Edward's room was slightly ajar, and through the crack, I could see his small figure sitting in the chair. He looked so different—older, thinner, weaker. I had expected to feel anger, to feel the old resentment surge up, but instead, I felt something unexpected. Pity. Seeing him like this, so vulnerable, it was hard to reconcile this man with the monster I had held in my heart for so long. For a moment, I hesitated, wondering if I should turn around and leave, but something kept me rooted to the spot. Maybe it was the prayer I had said earlier, or maybe it was the whisper of forgiveness trying to find its way into my heart. For a moment, I hesitated, debating whether I should turn and walk away.

Alvin stepped forward and knocked gently on the door before we entered. Edward's eyes widened, and when they met mine, something unspoken passed between us. His face registered surprise, and we briefly stared at each other. The years of silence between us hung heavy in the air. I could see recognition in his eyes, but also confusion and perhaps guilt. He opened his mouth to say something, but no words came out. My throat tightened, and I swallowed hard, forcing myself to breathe. I had spent hours imagining this moment, rehearsing what I would say, how I would confront him—but now, standing here, all those rehearsals seemed pointless.

The silence lingered until Alvin finally spoke; he and Edward exchanged greetings, slipping almost effortlessly into the familiar rhythm they had shared in the years before I cut off all contact with him. Edward then turned to me and said, "I didn't expect to see you. I always figured if I ever got sick, you wouldn't bother to come." I met his gaze and replied, "I'm also surprised to be here." I explained that we came to check on him, meet with his doctors, and discuss his condition.

As we spoke, I could see Edward's expression soften, though he remained quiet. When the doctor came in a few moments later, I was grateful for the distraction. As he spoke about Edward's diagnosis and the severity of his illness, I felt a mix of emotions—grief, despair, and, strangely, empathy for the brother I had once loved. I also felt rage for the man who had hurt me, and an odd, unwelcome compassion for the frail figure sitting in the chair.

The doctor's words washed over me: tumor, inoperable, palliative care. They felt heavy, final. The man before me was not the boy who hurt me so many years ago, and yet they were one and the same. How could I reconcile that?

As the meeting with the doctor ended, Alvin stepped out of the room to give us privacy. I was left alone with Edward, though I wasn't sure what I would say. Edward looked at me, his eyes filled with something I couldn't quite place—regret, maybe, or remorse. I didn't know if I was ready to forgive him, or if I ever would be, but in that moment, I felt something shift. I realized that forgiveness wasn't for him; it was for me. It wasn't about excusing what he had done but about freeing myself from the pain that had bound me for so long.

The quietness between us felt heavy, almost suffocating. I searched his face, looking for answers to questions I wasn't sure I could voice. My heart pounded in my chest as I realized that if I didn't speak now, I might never have the chance. Summoning every ounce of courage, I broke the silence. We need to talk," I said, my voice steady despite the storm of emotions brewing inside me. "Why did you do those things to me when I was a little girl?"

He didn't flinch, didn't ask what I meant. He already knew. His eyes dropped to his hands, which fidgeted nervously in his lap. I could see the weight of my words pressing down on him, but I couldn't stop now. "Did anyone do anything to hurt you when you were a child?" I asked, my voice gentler but still insistent.

For a moment, he said nothing. The seconds stretched on, and I thought perhaps he wouldn't answer. But then, in a voice barely above a whisper, he said, "I don't know, except that my cousins were doing it to each other, so I did it to you. And I'm sorry. I was wrong."

His words hung in the air, and for a moment, I felt an overwhelming wave of anger. "I don't know" felt insufficient, hollow. How could he not know? But as I looked at him—this frail man sitting before me, I saw something else. I saw shame. I saw guilt. And I saw a brokenness that mirrored my own.

I don't know what came over me, but without hesitation, I responded, "I forgive you." The words felt foreign as they left my lips, as though they belonged to someone else. And yet, the moment they were spoken, I felt a strange lightness, as if a weight I had carried for decades had suddenly been lifted.

Edward looked up at me, his eyes wide with surprise. "You do?" he asked, his voice cracking. "Yes," I said, the conviction in my voice surprising me. "I forgive you. Not because what you did was okay—it wasn't. But because I can't carry this anymore. It's been too heavy for too long."

He nodded slowly, tears welling in his eyes. "I don't deserve it," he said, his voice trembling. "Maybe not," I replied, my tone resolute but not unkind. "But forgiveness isn't about what you deserve. It's about what I deserve. And I deserve to heal."

The room grew quiet again, but this time, the silence felt different. It wasn't heavy or oppressive; it was peaceful, almost soothing. For the first time in years, I felt a sense of closure, a feeling that I had taken back something that had been stolen from me.

"I'm sorry," he said again, his voice softer this time, almost pleading. "I can't undo what I did, but I'm so sorry." "I know," I said. And in that moment, I realized that I truly did. I couldn't change the past, couldn't erase the pain he had caused me, but I could choose to stop letting it define me. Forgiving him didn't mean forgetting, and it certainly didn't mean excusing his actions. It meant reclaiming my power, my peace, and my future.

"It is during our darkest moments
that we must focus to see the light."

— Aristotle

CHAPTER II

The Emotional Struggle

*Come to me, all you who are weary
and burdened, and I will
give you rest.*

~ Matthew 11:28 (NIV)

The moment when I first stepped inside Edward's hospital room and saw he was no longer the figure of power he once was, something cracked in me. I was an adult now, yet in that instant, I felt like a young girl again, standing in the presence of someone who had shaped my past in ways I was only beginning to fully comprehend.

Trauma has a way of defying time. It doesn't remain confined to the past; it threads itself into the present, shaping the way I move through life in ways I sometimes don't even recognize. It is in the way I hesitate before trusting, in the way I scrutinize people's words, always searching for an unspoken threat. I had spent years learning how to live around my pain rather than through it, but when I sat beside Edward, I realized that avoidance was no longer an option.

The days following my first visit were filled with reflection. That hospital room had become a battleground where my past and present collided in ways I hadn't expected. I had walked into that room believing I was in control, believing I could set the terms of my emotions. But trauma doesn't abide by rationality. It moves as it pleases, showing up when least expected, unraveling the carefully built walls of survival.

I replayed our conversation over and over in my mind, scrutinizing his expressions, searching for sincerity in his words. Was he truly sorry, or was his apology a final grasp at redemption? I wanted to believe that it mattered, that his remorse could shift something in me, but the truth was, I wasn't sure it did. Forgiveness had always felt like surrender, as if by offering it, I would be letting go of something that had defined my survival. I had lived inside my anger for so long, I wasn't sure who I would be without it.

As I replayed the visit in my mind, there were moments when I felt nothing but rage. I saw myself sitting beside his bed, watching how his hands trembled as he reached for water, listening to the rhythmic beeping of the monitors, and I wanted to scream. How could he lie there, weak and dependent, when he had once held so much power over me? How was it fair that I had spent my life carrying the weight of what he had done, only for him to slip into sickness, into fragility, into the arms of sympathy? I wanted justice, but what does justice look like when time has already stolen the opportunity for retribution?

I questioned everything. How could someone I once trusted hurt me so deeply? Was this some kind of test from God? Had I really carried this weight for so long without breaking? And the most agonizing question of all: What did healing even look like?

Each visit reopened wounds I wasn't sure how to close. There were nights when I lay awake, staring at the ceiling, replaying memories that felt too close, too real. The past had a way of pressing itself into the present, demanding to be acknowledged. But I wasn't sure I was ready. Healing felt like a far-off concept, something reserved for those who had fully let go. And I wasn't sure I wanted to let go.

Somewhere deep inside, I still carried the belief that I was to blame. It didn't matter how much I intellectually knew it wasn't true—the feeling still existed, still whispered in the quiet moments when doubt crept in. It was a cruel paradox: I knew I had done nothing wrong, yet I felt like I had failed. Failed to stop it, failed to speak up sooner, failed to protect myself in a way that hindsight made seem so simple.

Shame was a quiet, constant presence, creeping into my thoughts and making me question my worth. It had lived inside of me for so long that I didn't know who I was without it. It told me that what happened to me made me damaged, that I was unworthy of protection, that I would always be the girl who wasn't believed, the girl who didn't matter enough to be saved. I knew, logically, that shame belonged to him, not to me, but knowing and believing are two different things.

I resented how much space he still took up in my mind. Even now, when I had built a life of my own, he lingered like a shadow, appearing in unexpected ways, making me doubt my strength, my ability to move beyond him. I hated that he still had that power, even from a hospital bed, even as he lay there weak and vulnerable. It felt unfair that I had to be the one to carry all the pain, to be the one grappling with emotions I never asked for.

And yet, beneath the rage, beneath the shame, there was something else. A grief that I didn't fully understand. I wasn't grieving Edward, at least not in the way his friends and doctors were. I was grieving the childhood I had lost, the innocence that had been stolen from me. I was grieving the relationships that had been shaped by my inability to trust, the moments of joy I had denied myself because I didn't believe I deserved them.

There were moments when I felt a flicker of something that confused me—a memory of Edward before the darkness, before he became the person who hurt me. I remembered the way he used to lift me onto his shoulders, making me feel like I could touch the sky. I remembered how he used to protect me from the outside world, and the cruel contradiction that he had also been the one I needed protecting from. These memories did not fit together, and I hated how much they haunted me.

I had spent my life compartmentalizing, keeping the pain separate from everything else, but now, it was all blending together. I didn't know how to reconcile these versions of Edward—the brother who had once cared for me and the one who had betrayed me in the worst way. How could both be true? And if they were, what did that mean for me?

Talking about it felt impossible. Even Alvin, as much as he loved me, could never fully understand the depth of what I was feeling. Trauma is a language that only those who have lived it can speak fluently. And even then, finding the right words can feel like an impossible task. How do you explain the way time bends around old wounds, making them feel fresh no matter how many years have passed? How do you articulate the invisible scars that dictate your every reaction, every moment of self-doubt, every impulse to run even when you are safe?

For weeks the emotional struggle was relentless. It felt like I was constantly walking a tightrope between resentment and obligation, between anger and guilt. I wanted to hate him, to let that anger consume me, but then I would see him struggling to lift a spoon to his mouth, and I would feel pity. I didn't want to feel pity. It felt like another betrayal of myself, of the little girl who had suffered in silence.

The weight of it all was suffocating. I wanted an answer, a way to resolve this tangled mess of emotions, but there wasn't one. There was only the reality of each day, of each choice to keep showing up, even when it hurt. I didn't know what healing looked like. But I knew I couldn't stay where I was. I had to keep moving forward, even if it was just one step at a time.

CHAPTER III

The Perfect Storm

> *You can't go back and change the*
> *beginning, but you can start where you*
> *are and change the ending.*
>
> ~ C.S. Lewis

The damaging combination of conditions that led to my childhood experience of abuse originated in the circumstances of my parents' marriage. My father, a 28-year-old Marine, and my mother, just 16 at the time, joined into a union marked by youth and inexperience. Both faced responsibilities far beyond their years. By the age of 31, my mother had given birth to seven children. Her first, Edward, was born when she was just 15, before she met my father. This rapid transition into adulthood left little room for self-reflection or healing from their own childhood traumas, which inevitably shaped the patterns in our home.

The 12-year age gap between my parents meant they were at vastly different stages of maturity when they married. My mother, still a teenager, lacked the life experience and emotional tools to navigate a turbulent marriage and a growing family. My father, though technically an adult, was also finding his footing, and their relationship became a fragile balancing act under the weight of societal and familial expectations.

My childhood was fragmented, not only by the abuse I suffered at the hands of my brother but also by the turmoil of my parents' separation, driven by domestic violence. My mother, exhausted by years of physical altercations, made the difficult decision to leave North Carolina and move to California, leaving her seven children, ranging in age from 4 to 19, behind. At the time, I was 9 years old and unaware of her reasons for leaving. I believe she wanted to bring her children with her to California, but she had limited income from her role as a part-time bus driver and waitress at a restaurant. Realistically, she lacked the financial resources to care for all of us on her own.

What outwardly appeared to be an act of self-preservation was likely her only option to prevent her children from living in poverty. Regardless of the reasoning, the rationale was not understood by children who just wanted their mother to be available. My siblings and I were raised by our father, a highly unusual arrangement for a man in the 1970s and still uncommon today. While my mother's move may have been necessary in her eyes, it left us in an environment ill-equipped to address our emotional needs.

The domestic violence that led to my mother's departure lingered like a shadow, even after she was gone. My father, a weekend alcoholic, used drinking as a coping mechanism. Though he ensured that we had food, shelter, and clothing, his focus on our material needs came at the expense of not recognizing the deeper issues within our family. His emotional detachment created gaps that we did not know how to fill, leaving wounds that would take years to acknowledge, let alone heal.

My mother's absence, whether intended for our well-being or not, added to the instability. The decision she made had a lasting impact on the children she left behind. And in that impact, the reasons no longer mattered—the absence was simply felt.

With my mother gone, the eldest siblings took on the role of surrogate parents, while the younger ones, like me, were left emotionally adrift. Though she may have made the best decision she could under the circumstances, our young minds could not grasp the complexities of financial hardship and survival. What we understood was that she was not there. There was little room for nurturing or open conversations about feelings. Survival became the priority—keeping the household running was more important than acknowledging the pain simmering beneath the surface. No one had the emotional bandwidth to unpack what we had lost, nor did we have the tools to process the dynamics that shaped our fractured family.

Without a unifying force, my siblings and I navigated our struggles separately. The older children were consumed with trying to fill the gaps left by our parents, while the younger ones were left to fend for themselves emotionally. This fragmentation masked the harm that was unfolding.

In a household where hierarchy was emphasized, Edward's position as an older sibling meant his authority over his younger siblings went unchecked. An unspoken rule of silence shielded his behavior, as we were discouraged from questioning authority. This environment made it nearly impossible for me to speak out. I feared his retaliation and doubted anyone would believe me.

My father's parenting style, influenced by his upbringing and military background, was strict and authoritarian. He emphasized control over connection, expecting us to adhere to rigid standards of discipline. While his intention may have been to create structure, the result was an environment where emotions were suppressed, and critical problems went unnoticed. Edward's behavior thrived in this setting. Silence was enforced, making it easier to ignore the intricacies of what was happening within our home.

The stigma surrounding domestic violence in the 1970s compounded our situation. My mother's decision to leave was seen as shameful rather than courageous. Her absence left us vulnerable to the forces that allowed harm to persist unnoticed. Societal norms of the time also played a role—discussions about abuse, mental health, and domestic violence were rare. Families were expected to present a united front, adhering to the mantra, "what happens in our household stays in our household." This cultural backdrop made it easy for my struggles to go overlooked.

As a child, I was a loner, often retreating to my room with books and music as my escape. Although I had a few friends, my father's strict rules forbade sleepovers or "hanging out in the streets." What he didn't realize was that the true danger—Edward—was within our home. Books and music became my refuge, a way to escape the chaos around me. However, this solitude also isolated me further. My father mistook my quietness for compliance, never suspecting the pain I carried in silence.

The combination of my father's inflexibility, my mother's absence, and broader societal expectations created the perfect storm for harm to go unnoticed. Each factor alone might not have been enough, but together they wove a web of silence and denial that allowed Edward's actions to persist.

It took years to untangle the layers of my childhood and understand how these forces shaped my life. The perfect storm wasn't the result of any single person or incident but rather a culmination of circumstances that left me at risk for harm.

Today, as I reflect on these events, I see the importance of ending the cycle of abuse. Sharing my story sheds light on the hidden harm that can exist within families and the need for open conversations about difficult topics. So many years were lost in silence, but it's only by breaking that silence that true healing can begin.

The lessons from my childhood continue to inform my journey of healing and forgiveness. By understanding the confluence of factors that shaped my experiences, I've found the clarity and strength to move forward. Though the scars remain, I'm learning to transform the pain into purpose. The challenges of my past may have shaped me, but they will not define my future.

Ending the cycle isn't just about acknowledging the damage—it's about actively choosing to do things differently. It's about becoming aware of the patterns that have shaped me and the lives of those before me and then making the conscious decision to disrupt them. This is where true change begins, not just for me, but for anyone caught in the same toxic loop. Although ending the cycle is not easy—it requires a deep commitment to understanding what has held us captive for so long. It requires confronting painful truths, even when the temptation to turn away is strong. The forward steps for me are about doing the hard work of breaking those patterns and discovering the freedom that lies on the other side.

"Nobody escapes being wounded.
We all are wounded people, whether physically,
emotionally, mentally, or spiritually."

— Henri J. M. Nouwen

CHAPTER IV

Through a Different Lens

*When we begin to see others through
the lens of their wounds rather than
their mistakes, we find the compassion
that leads to true understanding.*

~ Unknown

For most of my life, I have only seen Edward through one lens—the lens of the pain he had caused me. It was the only way I knew how to see him. He wasn't my brother; he was my abuser. He wasn't family; he was a wound that had never fully healed. But sitting by his hospital bed, watching him grow weaker each day, I found myself questioning the absoluteness of that perspective. Was he only the sum of his worst actions? Could I acknowledge the damage he had done to me while also recognizing the pain he had carried long before he ever hurt me?

I wasn't looking to absolve him. Forgiveness did not require me to rewrite history or diminish the suffering he had inflicted. But as I sat beside him in those final days, I found myself looking at him through a different lens—one that forced me to confront uncomfortable truths. Edward had not been born into a world of love and security. His wounds, though no justification for his actions, had been etched into him long before he etched pain into me.

Edward spent most of his childhood being raised by our grandmother. When our mother first married my father, she did not bring Edward into her new home right away. He was left behind, watching from a distance as she built a life with a new husband, new children, and a home that did not yet have space for him. I tried to imagine what that must have felt like for a young boy—to be old enough to understand that you had been left behind, yet too young to fully grasp why.

By the time Edward finally came to live with us, he was a teenager, and the damage had already been done. There is a certain loneliness that attaches itself to a child who has spent years feeling like an outsider to their own family. I had never considered before how that loneliness might have shaped him. How it might have hardened him, made him feel disconnected, made him question his place in the world.

My father treated Edward as his own son, never making a distinction between him and his biological children. However, my father's attitude and behavior could not erase the years Edward had spent feeling like an afterthought. And then there was the absence of his own biological father—an absence that left a void he never had the chance to fill. What does it do to a boy to grow up without ever knowing his father? What does it do to him to watch his mother start a new life without him? Did he wonder why he wasn't included sooner? Did he question whether he was truly wanted? Did he feel abandoned?

As I sat in that hospital room, I thought about the things I had never asked about. I thought about the things I had never allowed myself to question because it was easier to see Edward as one-dimensional. It was easier to keep him in a box labeled "abuser" and never examine the parts of him that existed outside of that label.

I had to acknowledge something I had never admitted to myself: Edward had been a victim, too. A victim of a fractured family, of abandonment, of circumstances that left him vulnerable to his own darkness. That did not excuse what he had done, but it did complicate the way I saw him. Then there was the reality of our parents' marriage.

As an adult, I came to understand that domestic violence was a steady presence in our home—a shadow that affected us all in ways I couldn't fully grasp as a child. At the time, I didn't have the language or awareness to name what was happening, but I've since learned how deeply those early experiences can imprint themselves on us. Even so, I hold onto memories of lighter moments—pizza parties, trips to the county fair, afternoons at the park with my siblings. Those snapshots of joy existed alongside a more complicated reality I couldn't see clearly back then. I often wonder what Edward experienced during those same years. Did he witness more than I did?

Did the violent behavior he observed leave its mark on him, shaping his understanding of power, love, or control? I tried to imagine what it must have been like for him, growing up in a house where love and violence coexisted in the same space. Was he afraid? Did he feel powerless? Did he learn, from an early age, that power meant control and control meant survival? Had he watched the same fights, the same cycles of hurt, and come to believe that harm was inevitable?

Maybe Edward never learned what love was supposed to be. Maybe he never learned how to exist in a world where love did not come with suffering. Maybe the anger that lived inside of him, the anger that eventually turned into harm, had started as something else—pain, fear, confusion.

I was not looking for excuses. I could not excuse him. I could not erase what he had done to me. But I could no longer pretend that his story had started with me. I had been his victim, but before that, he had been a boy in pain.

It was a difficult truth to accept. For so long, I had wanted to believe that what he did was purely an act of cruelty, that he had made a choice to hurt me, and that choice had nothing to do with anything else. But now, I had to wonder: Was it a choice at all, or was it the only way he knew how to exert control over a life where he had once felt powerless?

Edward had been involved in several relationships, but he was never married. I don't know if he ever truly experienced love or if he ever felt like he belonged within our family structure. Though we never labeled ourselves as half-siblings, I often wondered if he carried that distinction in his heart. Did he ever feel like an outsider among us, even as we treated him as one of our own? Did he ever feel like he fully belonged? Or did that early rejection plant a seed that made him feel as though he was always standing on the outside looking in?

There were moments when I felt guilty for even considering these thoughts. How could I let myself feel compassion for him? How could I sit there, knowing what he had taken from me, and allow myself to wonder what had been taken from him?

But as difficult as it was, I couldn't deny what I saw when I looked at him now. He was no longer the powerful figure I had feared. He was a man fading away, a man at the end of his life, grappling with his own regrets, his own pain. For the first time, I wondered if he had ever wanted to tell me the truth—if he had ever wanted to say more than his apology, if he had ever wanted to admit that he, too, had been shaped by things he couldn't control. I would never know.

It was unsettling watching someone who had once hurt me so deeply become so defenseless. Had I not known him, had he been a stranger, I might have pitied him. But knowing what I knew, pity was tangled with too much resentment, too much history. Still, something in me softened.

Not in a way that erased what had happened, but in a way that allowed me to see him as something more than just my pain. I saw him as flawed, as damaged, as shaped by wounds that came long before me. It didn't make what he did right. But it made him human.

I had spent my life seeing Edward as a monster, but now, I could see him as something more complicated. He was broken, just like me. He had carried pain, just like me. He had been hurt, just like me. And in that realization, I felt something shift inside of me. I was no longer looking at him as my abuser. I was looking at him as a man—one who had made terrible choices, but also one who had suffered in ways I would never fully understand.

Perhaps this was forgiveness. Not in the way people often imagined it—not as an absolution, not as a dismissal of pain—but as a quiet acknowledgment of truth. The truth that hurt people hurt people. That cycles of pain don't begin and end with one person. That healing is not just about letting go—it is about understanding, even when understanding feels impossible.

I would never know the full weight of Edward's pain. I would never know if he had wanted to be different, if he had wished he had made different choices. But what I did know was that his story had never been simple. And neither was mine.

We are commanded to seek out those who are lost.

We are to be our brother's keeper.

—Joseph B. Wirthlin

CHAPTER V

My Brother's Keeper: The Choice to Care

*Be kind and compassionate
to one another, forgiving each other,
just as in Christ God forgave you.*

~ Ephesians 4:32

When Edward's health declined, I faced a pivotal choice: should I, as his sibling, step into the role of caregiver? This decision was laden with conflicting emotions. On one hand, there was a sense of familial obligation, a societal expectation that family members care for one another in times of need. On the other hand, the memories of past abuses loomed large, casting shadows over any inclination to assist.

Caring for a sibling who has caused profound personal harm is a journey fraught with emotional complexity. My decision to care for Edward, despite our painful history, was not made lightly. I had to confront deep-seated emotions, reconcile a sense of familial duty with personal pain, and navigate the turbulent waters of forgiveness and self-preservation.

Assuming the role of caregiver for Edward unearthed a myriad of emotions—resentment, anger, and sadness—that I had long tried to suppress. Each act of care reopened old wounds, challenging my emotional resilience.

Research indicates that caregivers who have experienced abuse by the person they are caring for often face heightened psychological distress. A study published in the *Journal of Interpersonal Violence* found that individuals in such situations exhibited higher levels of depressive symptoms compared to caregivers without a history of abuse.

The act of caregiving became a double-edged sword. While it provided me with an opportunity to demonstrate compassion and perhaps find closure, it also served as a constant reminder of past traumas. Balancing these conflicting emotions required a commitment to personal healing.

My internal conflict between a sense of duty and personal pain was perhaps the most challenging aspect of this journey. The unspoken cultural and familial expectations dictated that I should care for my ailing brother, yet my personal experiences screamed for self-preservation.

This dichotomy is not uncommon among individuals in similar situations. The pressure to uphold family responsibilities can lead to feelings of guilt and shame, especially when personal boundaries are at stake. It's a delicate balance between honoring one's values and protecting one's mental and emotional well-being.

Forgiveness emerged as a central theme in my journey. To provide genuine care, I needed to commit to my pledge to forgive Edward for the pain he had caused. However, forgiveness is a complex and deeply personal process.

It's important to recognize that forgiveness does not equate to condoning harmful behavior. Instead, it involves releasing the hold that past hurts have on one's present life. This process can lead to personal liberation, allowing individuals to move forward without the burden of resentment.

Establishing clear boundaries was crucial in managing my caregiving relationship with Edward. Given our history, it was essential to define what I was comfortable with and to communicate these limits effectively.

Setting boundaries is a vital aspect of caregiving, especially when past abuse is involved. It helps protect the caregiver's well-being and ensures that the act of caring does not become a source of further emotional harm. This might involve delegating certain tasks to others, limiting time spent in triggering environments, or seeking external support when needed. Unfortunately, in my case, I didn't have the option of asking another family member to step in to assist in caring for Edward. It was just me, and the realization was stressful.

While Mary and Arthur Jr. provided emotional support, they didn't have the capacity to help with visits or interface with the medical team. Their encouragement was meaningful, but when it came to the exhausting demands of hospital visits, medical decisions, and advocating for Edward's care, I was alone. There was no one else to share the weight of responsibility, no one to take over when the emotional toll became overwhelming. The lack of hands-on support made setting boundaries even more crucial—if I didn't protect myself, no one else would.

Therapy became a refuge, a place where I could lay down the emotional weight I carried and begin to untangle the complexities of my past and present. My counselor helped me navigate the contradictions of caregiving—how I could extend care without compromising my own well-being, how I could hold space for my pain while still showing up for Edward. There were moments when I hesitated to fully share my thoughts, fearing that even in a professional setting, my emotions would be too difficult to explain. But over time, I allowed myself to be vulnerable, to speak the truths I had kept buried for so long.

Despite the challenges, this experience also became an opportunity for personal growth. Caring for Edward forced me to confront unresolved emotions, leading to a deeper understanding of myself and my capacity for compassion.

Caring for someone who had caused me harm highlighted the complexity of human relationships and the resilience of the human spirit. While the process was fraught with difficulty, it also paved the way for healing and personal development.

The decision to care for Edward, despite our painful past, was a profound journey through emotional turmoil, internal conflict, and ultimately, personal growth. It underscored the importance of setting boundaries, seeking support, and engaging in self-reflection. This experience gave me a deeper understanding of compassion, forgiveness, and the strain associated with the call of familial duty.

CHAPTER VI

Unfinished Conversations: What Was Left Unsaid

Closure isn't always about the final conversation; sometimes, it's about accepting what was left unsaid and choosing to move forward anyway.

~ Unknown

Throughout the weeks of Edward's hospitalization, I found myself sitting at his bedside nearly every day. As the days turned into a month, there were so many moments when I sat beside Edward, wanting—aching—to tell him the truth. I wanted him to know the weight of what he had done, how his actions had altered the course of my life in ways I was still working to untangle.

I wanted to look him in the eye and ask if he even understood the depth of the wounds he left behind. Did he ever think about the little girl he betrayed? Did he ever wonder how his choices shaped the woman I became? The words sat at the edge of my tongue so many times, but I swallowed them down, uncertain of what they would accomplish.

Instead, I talked about the weather, the hospital food, the noise from the hallway. I kept the conversations light, filling the space with surface-level words that masked the storm inside me. I redirected his attention when his thoughts drifted to the pain of his illness, doing my best to offer some measure of comfort in his final days. But inside, I was wrestling with a different kind of pain, a kind he would never fully grasp. There was so much I wanted to say, but I knew I never would.

I wanted to tell him how much he had hurt me, how his actions left scars that I spent years trying to heal. I wanted him to understand that his betrayal didn't just steal my childhood innocence—it robbed me of my sense of safety, of my ability to trust, of the dream of having an older brother who protected me rather than preyed on me. I wanted to scream at him for the anxiety I battled, for the deep-rooted insecurities that made me question my worth, for the way I pushed myself to over-achieve at the expense of my own mental peace—because if I was excelling, maybe I could prove I was more than what happened to me.

I wanted to tell him that he missed out—on so much. On family dinners filled with laughter. On birthdays and holidays that came and went without him. On watching my daughter Chantell grow into the strong, brilliant woman she became, on being a good uncle to my nieces.

I wanted to tell him that he could have had a place at the table, but he chose to forfeit it when he betrayed me. That he missed out on hanging out with Alvin, watching football, drinking beers, and having conversations about life. That he never got to celebrate the academic achievements of my grandchildren, Bryce and Brooklyn, who were growing into such bright, promising young people.

But I didn't say any of it. As much as I wanted to, I couldn't bring myself to voice those words. And the strangest part? I didn't hold back out of fear—I held back because I didn't want to hurt him. It was an odd realization, considering the pain he had caused me. I had every right to unleash my anger, to demand acknowledgment, to lay bare the damage he had done. But in those final days, sitting beside his frail body, watching as life drained from him, I couldn't bring myself to add more suffering to his last moments.

So I leaned into my faith. I focused on making him comfortable, on being present without bringing up the past. I prayed for him silently, asking God to grant him peace, to grant me peace, to fill the space between us with something other than pain. I reminded myself that this was the path I chose—not for him, but for me. Choosing compassion did not mean excusing his actions; it meant that I refused to let the past consume me any longer.

Faith became my anchor in those moments. When resentment threatened to rise, I prayed. When I wanted to tell him everything, I reminded myself that God already knew my pain. I found solace in the belief that I had been heard that I had been seen, and that healing did not require Edward's acknowledgment. My healing had already begun long before I sat beside him in that hospital room.

There were moments when I questioned if I was doing the right thing. Was I betraying myself by choosing silence? Was I letting him off too easily? But as I looked at him—this man who had once held power over me, now reduced to a frail body fighting for breath—I realized that no words could undo the past. No confrontation could erase what had happened. What mattered was that I was no longer bound by it.

Keeping our conversations light didn't mean I had forgotten. It didn't mean I had forgiven him in the way people often expect forgiveness to look. It meant that I had freed myself from needing anything from him—an apology, an explanation, a moment of reckoning. My healing was no longer contingent on his response. That was the most powerful realization of all.

I sat with him, sometimes in silence, sometimes in laughter, sometimes in shared memories that felt safe to recall. I watched as he faded, as his body weakened, as the weight of his own regrets seemed to settle in. I knew he had his own unfinished conversations, words he probably wanted to say but never would.

At times, I wondered if he sensed it—the things I wasn't saying, the truths I kept locked inside. If he did, he never acknowledged it. And maybe that was for the best. Maybe we both understood, in our own unspoken way, that some things could never be fully reconciled.

In the end, I chose grace. Not for him, but for myself. I chose to leave the things unsaid, not because they didn't matter, but because I refused to let them define me any longer. I chose to close this chapter in a way that brought me peace, not in a way that would leave me with more regret.

Sitting beside him in his final moments, I realized that I no longer needed him to understand my pain for me to move forward. That was the unfinished conversation I had been searching for all along—the one I had with myself.

CHAPTER VII

Learning to Love the Unlovable

> *To love means*
> *loving the unlovable.*
>
> ~ C. K. Chesterton

C aring for the well-being of others is embedded in my soul. For nearly forty years, I have dedicated my life to serving the community that includes at-risk children and families, standing in the gap for those who had no one to advocate for them. I have fought for justice, comforted the hurting, and extended grace to those society often deems unworthy.

So, when it came to caring for Edward, it would have been unnatural—out of character—for me to ignore his suffering. Even with our painful history, I could not turn my back on him. He was dying, and the thought of him leaving this world alone, without care or dignity, was something I could not allow. Despite the deep wounds he had inflicted upon me, I saw his humanity. And through the grace of God, I found the strength to offer him the love and care he needed in his final days.

There were moments when loving Edward came easily, moments when I could remember the brother who laughed loudly and called me

"Miss Hollywood" for my ever-changing hairstyles and sense of style. I could remember his booming voice filling a room, his jokes making others chuckle, and how he could light up a space when he was at ease.

Those memories did not erase the pain he caused me, but they did remind me that he, too, was a human being—a flawed and broken one, like all of us. It was in those fleeting moments that I could see him not just as the person who hurt me, but as someone in desperate need of love and compassion. I didn't have to condone his past actions to acknowledge his suffering in the present. I didn't have to excuse him to extend kindness. God didn't call me to rewrite history; He called me to walk in love. And that love meant ensuring Edward was not abandoned in his final days.

There were also moments when loving him was difficult, when the weight of my own pain sat heavy on my chest. There were days when I questioned why I was the one chosen to care for him, why the responsibility of his dignity in death had fallen on me. But I knew that resisting the call to compassion would only deepen the wounds within me. I could not heal by holding on to anger; I could not find peace while withholding love. Even when I did not fully understand my "why," I trusted that God was working through me. He was teaching me to surrender my bitterness so I could walk in true freedom. God was not asking me to forget—I would never forget—but He was asking me to release. In surrendering my pain, I was able to give Edward a piece of the peace I carried within.

Without hesitation, I cared for him in the ways I knew best. When he was uncomfortable, I rubbed his head and held his hand. I made sure he had company when I could not be there, even paying others to sit with him so he would not be alone. I spoke to doctors and nurses on his behalf, making sure his needs were met with dignity. Every act of care I extended was not just for him, but for the person I had become.

I could not allow my heart to be hardened by the pain of the past. Loving the unlovable was not about deserving; it was about obedience to the call God placed on my life. It was about showing grace even when it felt undeserved. And in doing so, I freed myself from the prison of resentment.

At first, I thought I was simply fulfilling my duty as a human services professional—stepping in to help someone in need. But I now realize that God was doing something much deeper in me. He was using this moment to heal wounds I didn't even know still existed. He was showing me that love is not always about emotion; sometimes, it is a choice we make despite how we feel. Love is the act of seeing someone's humanity, even when they have failed to honor yours. It is extending kindness when the world says you have every right to turn away. It is holding space for healing, not just for the other person but for yourself.

In loving Edward, I was not just giving him something he needed—I was also receiving something my soul had been longing for. A release, a letting go, a newfound peace that could only come from choosing compassion over resentment.

Forgiveness and love are deeply intertwined. There were moments I still had to wrestle with my pain, moments when old wounds threatened to resurface. But I knew that the path I had chosen—this path of love— was the only one that could bring me true healing. God did not call me to carry the weight of my hurt forever. Instead, He called me to lay it down at His feet, to trust that He would turn my pain into purpose. And He did. In learning to love Edward in his weakest state, I learned to love myself more deeply. I learned that I was stronger than my wounds, that my capacity for grace was bigger than my history. And through that love, I stepped fully into the healing God had been preparing for me all along.

Loving the unlovable does not mean forgetting the pain they caused. It does not mean pretending the past did not happen or silencing the parts of me that once cried out for justice. Instead, it means choosing to see beyond the wounds, to recognize that every person—no matter how broken—was once a child, shaped by their own pain and circumstances. Edward had his own story, though it did not excuse his actions. He was a man who had made choices that deeply hurt others, including me. But in his final days, he was just a man facing his mortality, unguarded and alone. I could have walked away, justified in my anger and grief. But something inside me—something God had placed there long ago—would not let me turn away from his suffering.

It was not an act of weakness to care for him; it was an act of strength. The world might say that love should be reserved for those who deserve it, but God calls us to something greater. He calls us to love even when it is difficult, even when it feels unfair. And so, I made the conscious choice to love Edward in the ways I could. I ensured that he was not abandoned in his final moments. I saw his suffering and did what I had always done—advocated, nurtured, and cared. This was not just about him; it was about who I was at my core. God had woven compassion into my very being, and I could not deny it, even in this most difficult of circumstances.

There were times when I wondered if Edward understood the depth of what I was doing for him. Did he see the sacrifice in my love? Did he feel the weight of my choice to stand by him despite everything? Perhaps he did, or perhaps he was too weak, too consumed by his own pain to grasp it fully. But it did not matter, because love is not always about being acknowledged. Love is about giving, even when there is nothing in return. Love is about obedience to the call placed on our hearts. And I knew that my purpose was not dependent on Edward's response but on my willingness to surrender to God's will.

I know now that my love for Edward in those final days reflected the love God has for all of us. None of us are truly deserving, yet He pours out grace and mercy upon us daily. He sees our worst moments, our greatest failures, and still calls us His own. He does not love us because we are perfect; He loves us because we are His. And if I am to walk in His image, I must love in that way too. I must love beyond reason, beyond my pain, beyond my own understanding. It was not my job to determine what Edward deserved—it was simply my job to show up with love. And in doing so, I found myself becoming more like the person God always intended me to be.

Surrendering my anger was not easy, but it was necessary for my own peace. Carrying bitterness would have only prolonged my suffering, keeping me shackled to a past I could not change. Letting go did not mean erasing my history but rather refusing to let it define my future. I wanted peace, and peace required release. So, I leaned into God's strength, trusting that He would hold me up when my emotions threatened to pull me down. I prayed for the ability to love, even when my flesh resisted. And little by little, I felt the burden lift. The love I extended to Edward became an offering—not just for him, but for my own healing.

Each time I wiped his brow, adjusted his blankets, or sat in quiet presence, I felt something shift within me. I was not just easing his suffering; I was allowing my heart to heal. Love has a way of softening the hardened places within us, of restoring what pain has tried to destroy. My love for Edward freed me from the weight of resentment and opened a door to a deeper peace than I had ever known. I had spent so much of my life carrying the pain of what he had done. And in the end, it was love—love in its purest, most sacrificial form—that finally set me free.

I recognize the divine orchestration of it all. I see how God used this experience to refine me, to teach me a lesson about love that no sermon or scripture alone could have imparted. I see how He prepared my heart long before I ever knew I would have to make this choice. Every moment of my career, every child I had ever fought for, every family I had ever served—it was all leading me to this. To this moment of reckoning, where I would have to decide if I truly believed in the power of love and forgiveness. And I did. Even when it hurt. Even when it made no sense.

The world teaches us that love should be transactional, that it should be given only when it is earned. But God's love is unconditional, and He calls us to love in that same way. Not just when it is easy, not just when it is comfortable, but especially when it is hard. It is in those moments of difficulty that love is tested, refined, and proven to be real. I do not claim that loving Edward was simple. There were tears, there were prayers, there were moments when my heart resisted. But I loved him anyway, because love is not about worthiness—it is about grace. And in extending grace, I found my own heart being healed.

I do not regret the love I gave him, the care I showed, or the compassion I extended. If anything, I am grateful. Grateful that I did not allow my pain to dictate my actions. Grateful that I chose love over bitterness. Grateful that in his final days, he was not alone. And most of all, grateful that God used this experience to teach me that love—true, unconditional love—has the power to transform not just those who receive it, but those who give it as well.

CHAPTER VIII

The Weight That Wasn't Mine to Carry

For each will have to
bear his own load.

~ Galatians 6:5

I recognize now that the weight of Edward's pain and the challenges in his life were never mine to carry. But at the time, it was extremely difficult to separate my role as someone who cared from the overwhelming sense of responsibility I felt. Even though I had long since removed myself from his life, his suffering pulled at me in ways I wasn't prepared for. Before his illness, I had no contact with him, only receiving occasional updates from Mary about his life.

I knew things weren't great for him, but I never asked too many questions—I had created boundaries for my own well-being. And yet, when his condition worsened, and the reality of his circumstances came to light, I felt a weight press down on me. It wasn't my life, my choices, or my mistakes, but somehow, I felt accountable for the situation he was in.

Guilt crept in like an unwelcome visitor, whispering that I should have done more, that I should have been there.

His living conditions at the time of his illness were heartbreaking. I learned that his residence was infested with bedbugs and other insects, a place unfit for anyone, let alone someone in declining health. He had no stability, no real financial resources to fall back on, as he had spent much of his life working under-the-table jobs as a mover on long-haul trucks.

There was no retirement plan, no savings, no safety net. When he was hospitalized, messages from his associates flooded in, each one carrying an undertone of expectation—someone had to step in, and that someone should be me. They told me he couldn't go back to his home, that he needed care, structure, support. The problem was that they all wanted to unload their concerns onto me as if I were the only person left to solve his problems. I felt the familiar pull of obligation, the instinct to drop everything and fix his life. But deep down, I knew that I couldn't.

My first reaction was to go into overdrive. I began mapping out every possible scenario—how he would get treatment, where he would stay, what kind of transportation he would need. I was making calls, researching resources, trying to construct a future for him that he had never built for himself. It was as if I had stepped into a role I hadn't auditioned for, one where I was expected to clean up the mess of someone else's life.

But then, something in me hesitated. A voice inside me, quiet but firm, told me to slow down. I had spent years learning about healthy boundaries, about not letting other people's choices dictate my own well-being. And yet, here I was, on the verge of carrying a burden that wasn't mine to bear. I had to remind myself: I was there to help, not to take over his life.

That realization didn't come without struggle. I had to ask myself why I felt so compelled to carry his weight, why guilt was creeping in when I had done nothing wrong. Edward had made his choices. He had lived his life the way he saw fit, never once reaching out for my help. So why did I feel responsible for fixing what he had broken? That's the conundrum so many victims face—we carry guilt that doesn't belong to us. We question if we should have done more, if we should have stayed connected, if we should have tried harder to intervene. It is a cruel trick of the mind, making us believe we had power where we never did. The truth is, I could not have saved Edward from himself.

I struggled with the idea that I had abandoned him, even though I had protected myself. I had chosen my peace, my healing, and my own well-being, and that was not something to feel guilty about. But guilt is insidious. It makes you believe that love must always come with sacrifice, that to truly care means to lose yourself in the process. I had to actively fight against that belief.

Helping someone does not mean undoing the consequences of their choices. Compassion does not mean self-sacrifice. And love does not mean bearing the weight of another person's entire existence. I had to separate my empathy from my responsibility, to remind myself that offering care does not mean erasing the past.

The weight of his struggles was never mine to carry, but there were moments I still wanted to pick it up. Maybe it was because I had spent my career serving others, finding solutions where others saw dead ends. Maybe it was because I had been conditioned to nurture, to step in, to fill the gaps that others had left behind. But I was not just a human services professional in this situation—I was also a survivor. And as a survivor, my healing had to come first.

If I had allowed guilt to dictate my actions, I would have been pulled back into a dynamic that never served me. I had to remind myself that I was not responsible for saving Edward—I was only responsible for showing up with the love and kindness I had to give. And sometimes, that meant knowing when to step back.

Victims often feel an unspoken obligation to carry the weight of those who hurt them. We battle with the idea that if we don't step in, if we don't care, we are somehow just as cold as the ones who harmed us. But that is a lie. Setting boundaries does not make us unkind. Recognizing that we are not responsible for fixing others does not make us selfish. And choosing our own healing over someone else's chaos does not make us heartless. I had to sit with that truth. I had to remind myself that my worth was not determined by how much of Edward's pain I was willing to absorb. I could care without carrying. I could love without losing myself.

The guilt did not disappear overnight. It surfaced in quiet moments, whispering that I should have done more, that I should have found another way. But I had to counter those thoughts with truth. The truth was that Edward had lived his life in a way that led to certain consequences. The truth was that he had never asked for my help before his illness, and I was under no obligation to rescue him now. The truth was that my love for him did not need to come at the expense of my own peace. I was not abandoning him; I was simply choosing not to drown alongside him. And that was a choice I had every right to make.

In the end, I did what I could. I made sure he had care, that he was not alone, that his final days had dignity. But I did not take on his entire life as my own. That distinction was crucial. It was the difference between compassion and self-destruction, between love and obligation. I had spent too many years carrying burdens that did not belong to me. This time, I chose differently. I chose to help, but not at the cost of my own well-being. I chose to care, but not to carry. And in making that choice, I found a freedom I had never known before.

CHAPTER IX

The Power of Presence: Showing Up with Compassion

> *A truly compassionate attitude toward others does not change even if they behave negatively or hurt you.*
>
> ~ Dalai Lama

I n my visits to Edward in the hospital, my acts of compassion brought a smile to his face during a time when I knew he was scared. What I realized was that my presence at the hospital with him was likely more therapeutic than any prescription or treatment he could receive. There was something about being seen, being acknowledged, that no medication could replace. Despite the complexity of our past, despite the pain he had caused me, I recognized that no one should face suffering alone.

Edward was a man who had lived a hard life, made choices that led him down painful roads, and now, as his body failed him, he had no choice but to face the consequences. I could have left him to handle it all on his own. But something inside me knew that compassion was not about who deserved it—it was about what kind of person I wanted to be. Sitting there, watching his expression soften in the warmth of my presence, I knew I had made the right choice. Love, even in its simplest form, has the power to transform even the most broken of moments.

Because he was illiterate, I knew that he couldn't read the forms and understand the instructions—so I handled it for him. Not in a way to make him feel less intelligent, but in a way to make him feel supported. There was no judgment in my actions, no superiority, just an understanding that we all have areas where we need help. It made me think about how often we shame others for their shortcomings instead of extending a hand. How easy it is to belittle, to criticize, rather than to assist with grace. But we are all human, carrying burdens that others cannot see. To extend compassion does not mean excusing the past—it simply means choosing humanity over pride.

We each deserve compassion, even in the darkest times. Not because of our actions, but because suffering is universal, and no one should face it alone. Compassion does not mean ignoring the truth or pretending that harm never occurred. It means recognizing that pain does not define a person's worth. As I sat with Edward, I thought about how much of life is shaped by the moments when we choose to show up for others. Not because they have earned it, but because it is the right thing to do. Sometimes, presence alone is the most profound gift we can give. A hand to hold, a voice to comfort, a moment of acknowledgment—these are the things that bring light into the darkness.

Showing up with compassion required me to lay down my expectations of how I thought things should be. I had to surrender my need for justice in that moment and embrace the simple act of being there. It wasn't about fixing his life, undoing the past, or making sense of what had happened between us. It was about recognizing that in this moment, he was a human being in need. And if I had the capacity to offer kindness, why should I withhold it? Compassion is not about what the other person deserves—it's about the character we choose to cultivate within ourselves. And in that room, I chose love over resentment.

The power of presence is that it does not require us to have all the answers—it simply asks that we show up. It asks that we bring our whole selves, flawed and uncertain, and offer what we can. Sometimes, that is enough. Sitting beside Edward, I saw the fear in his eyes, the uncertainty of what lay ahead. And I knew that if I could ease his suffering, even a little, then my presence had meaning.

There is a misconception that compassion is a weakness, that offering kindness to those who have hurt us is a betrayal of our own pain. But I have come to learn that compassion is a strength unlike any other. It takes courage to stand in the face of hurt and choose love instead of anger. It takes resilience to show up with an open heart when every part of you has been taught to guard it. Compassion is not about letting someone off the hook—it is about setting yourself free from the burden of bitterness. And in extending it, I found that I, too, was healing.

As I continued to show up for Edward, I found that my presence became a silent act of redemption—not for him, but for me. Each time I walked into that hospital room, I was reclaiming my power. Not by holding onto the past, but by choosing to create something new in the present. I could not rewrite what had happened, but I could decide what happened next. And what happened next was my choice, not his. My choice to love. My choice to forgive. My choice to be the person I wanted to be, regardless of what he had done.

The power of presence is that it does not demand perfection. It does not require that we have resolved all our feelings before we show up. It simply asks that we bring ourselves, as we are, and offer what we have.

That is enough. Compassion does not have to be grand or complicated. Sometimes, it is as simple as sitting beside someone, bearing witness to their humanity. Sometimes, it is a quiet reassurance that they are not alone. And in those moments, healing happens—not just for them, but for us as well.

Presence is more than just being physically there—it is about intentionality, about showing up with an open heart and a willingness to offer comfort. When I looked at Edward, I saw a man who had lived a life full of hardship, but in that hospital room, none of that mattered. What mattered was that he was human, and he needed care. I thought about all the times I had needed someone to see me, to acknowledge my pain, to simply be present in my suffering.

And I realized that in showing up for Edward, I was also honoring the moments when others had shown up for me. The cycle of love and compassion continues when we choose to participate in it. And in that hospital room, I chose to break the cycle of pain by stepping into the power of presence.

The greatest lesson I took from this experience was that compassion is a gift that holds the power to heal, to restore, and to bring peace where there was once pain. And as I sat with Edward, I knew that my presence reflected something far greater than myself. It reflected God's love, grace, and the ability to find beauty in even the most complicated relationships. In choosing to be present, I found a part of myself that I didn't know I needed. And that was the true power of showing up with compassion.

CHAPTER X

Quieting the Noise

> *Have the courage to follow your heart*
> *and intuition. They somehow*
> *already know what you truly*
> *want to become.*
>
> ~ Steve Jobs

When I made the decision to care for Edward, the reactions from those around me were as varied as they were intense. Many of my friends and family members were shocked. Some couldn't fathom why I would extend myself in such a profound way for someone who had caused me so much pain. The voices were loud and persistent, but amidst the chaos, there were those who stood beside me—Mary, my brother Arthur Jr., my daughter Chantell, and Alvin. Their support became my lifeline in a sea of disbelief. The comments ranged from mild curiosity to outright condemnation. Some asked, "Why would you do that?" Others admitted, "I could never do this." And then there were the ones who simply said, "I don't understand why you would be there for him."

Though part of me wasn't surprised by their reactions, the weight of their judgment still stung. It wasn't easy to hear people question my choice, especially when I knew it was the right thing for me. People were quick to assign meaning to my actions, often projecting their own experiences and emotions onto my decision. Their discomfort with my compassion reflected their own fears, their own unresolved pain. It was easier for them to judge than to try to understand. Some had been hurt in their own lives and couldn't imagine offering grace to someone who had wounded them. Others held onto rigid definitions of justice, believing that forgiveness had to be earned, that redemption was conditional. But my journey was my own, and I refused to let their limited perspectives define my path.

As I navigated these conversations, I realized that many of the criticisms stemmed from fear. Fear of vulnerability, fear of confronting one's own pain, and fear of stepping into the unknown. My decision to care for Edward wasn't just about him; it was about breaking the chains of fear and stepping into a place of spiritual freedom.

I understood that many people hold onto anger and resentment because it makes them feel safe, as if protecting their wounds means preventing further harm. But I had spent too many years bound by that way of thinking. God was calling me to something deeper—something that required me to trust in His plan more than my own emotions. This was my test of faith, and I knew I could not fail it by giving in to the expectations of others.

Initially, I wrestled with self-doubt. Could I truly handle the emotional toll of caring for Edward? The external voices only amplified my internal questions. But as I turned to prayer and reflection, I found clarity. God's purpose became my anchor, guiding me through the storm of opinions and doubt. I knew that I had been placed in this situation for a reason. And despite the discomfort, I was willing to walk this road because I believed in something greater than my pain—I believed in healing, in grace, in the power of love.

For me, this journey became deeply personal. It didn't revolve around seeking approval or validation from others. My decision centered on honoring God's purpose for my life and embracing my own healing. The act of stepping into this role wasn't just about helping him; it was about tuning out the noise of external opinions and heeding the gentle voice of faith within me. And in doing so, I reclaimed a piece of myself that had been lost in the shadows of the past.

Each day brought new challenges and new opportunities for growth. My role as a caregiver required me to confront the pain of the past while also embracing the hope of the future. It was a delicate balance, but one that brought profound healing. With each act of service, the chains of bitterness and resentment lightened. I wasn't just offering Edward comfort in his final days—I was also offering myself a chance to heal in ways I never thought possible. Love, I realized, was not just about what we give to others; it's about what we allow ourselves to receive in return.

There were moments when the noise became overwhelming. I had to learn how to protect my peace. This meant setting boundaries with those who couldn't respect my journey. It meant leaning into prayer and meditation, seeking solace in the stillness of God's presence. And it meant finding strength in the support of those who truly understood my heart. Not everyone needed to agree with my decision, but I needed to be at peace with it. And peace, I learned, is something we create from within—it is not granted by the approval of others.

One of the most challenging aspects of this journey was learning not to internalize the negativity. The doubts and criticisms of others had the potential to seep into my own thoughts if I wasn't careful. But through faith, I learned to distinguish between constructive feedback and destructive judgment. I held onto the truth that my actions were aligned with God's purpose, even if others couldn't see it. People often judge what they don't understand, and I had to remind myself that their disbelief was not my burden to bear. Their words did not define me—my faith did.

The tendency to judge others is often based on our own fears, life experiences, and lack of compassion. We see things through the lens of our own pain, and sometimes, that lens is distorted. Some people had never experienced the kind of deep healing that allows for radical compassion, so they couldn't comprehend my decision. Others were afraid to let go of their own grudges because doing so would require them to confront their pain. I recognized that their judgments weren't truly about me; they were about what my actions forced them to face within themselves. But I refused to let their fears become my own.

Ignoring the noise also meant embracing grace—not just for Edward, but for those who didn't understand my decision. I chose to see their reactions as an opportunity to extend compassion. Their disbelief was rooted in their own struggles, and I couldn't fault them for that. I chose to focus on God's purpose rather than the opinions of others. I preferred forgiveness over resentment, faith over fear, and love over judgment. That was the path I had chosen, and I would not stray from it, no matter how much others questioned my choices.

Mary was a constant source of encouragement. She reminded me that forgiveness isn't about excusing the past but about freeing ourselves from its grip. Her words resonated deeply, giving me the strength to move forward. Though she wished she could be there, Mary was unable to tolerate the long drive from Jacksonville to Greenville to see Edward because of her condition. Despite this, she remained present in other ways, offering unwavering emotional support. She understood the weight of my decision and never failed to acknowledge it. She knew I didn't owe Edward compassion or care after what he had done, yet she expressed deep gratitude for my choice to advocate for him in his final days. Her appreciation reinforced my resolve, reminding me that my actions weren't about what was deserved, but about who I chose to be.

Arthur Jr., too, stood by me with unwavering support. He knew the pain I carried and recognized the courage it took to face it head-on. Alvin's steady presence provided a sense of stability, a quiet reassurance that I wasn't alone in this journey. Chantell was intentional about checking in with me, making sure I had the space to process my emotions while still feeling supported. Together, they formed a circle of strength that helped me drown out the negativity around me, allowing me to focus on the path I had chosen—one of healing, faith, and forgiveness.

This chapter of my life taught me the power of resilience. It showed me that healing is full of unforeseen twists and turns. And it reminded me that the voices that truly matter are the ones that align with God's truth. I found that the act of giving brought its own rewards. It deepened my faith, strengthened my character, and brought a sense of peace that I hadn't known before. The noise of external opinions became a distant echo, replaced by the quiet assurance of God's presence.

The opinions of others don't define me; God's purpose does. True healing comes from within, guided by faith and love. Even during painful situations, there is beauty to be found in forgiveness and redemption, and I will always carry the lessons of this experience with me. I know that there will always be noise when choices made are controversial, but I also know that I have the strength to rise above it. With God's guidance, I can face any challenge and find peace amid chaos.

Whatever is in your path and in your heart

you need to do.

— J. Cole

Forgiveness and Understanding

Darkness cannot drive out darkness;

only light can do that.

Hate cannot drive out hate;

only love can do that.

— Martin Luther King, Jr.

CHAPTER XI

The Forgiveness Factor

> *Forgiveness does not change the past,*
> *but it does enlarge the future.*
>
> ~ Paul Boese

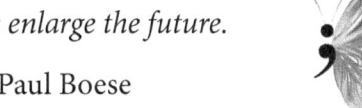

Forgiveness isn't a single act, nor is it a moment of profound realization or a grand gesture. It is a process—a series of choices made day by day, moment by moment. Some days, it felt within reach; other days, it seemed impossible. But I came to understand that forgiveness, like healing, was something I was doing for myself. It wasn't about excusing Edward's actions; it was about freeing myself from the prison of anger and resentment that had held me captive for so long.

At the same time, healing made forgiveness possible. When I was drowning in pain, when my wounds were still raw, forgiveness felt unattainable. It wasn't until I tended to my own hurt—through therapy, prayer, self-reflection, and setting boundaries—that I even considered it. Healing gave me the clarity to see that forgiveness wasn't about erasing the past but about refusing to let it control me. It allowed me to shift from victim to survivor, and eventually to someone who could view the past with understanding rather than anguish. It didn't mean the pain disappeared—the memories remained, and at times, they still hurt. But forgiveness gave me the strength to face those memories without being consumed by them.

I also realized that forgiveness required giving myself grace. For years, I had been my harshest critic, carrying the weight of blame that was never mine to bear. I blamed myself for not speaking up sooner, for not confronting Edward earlier, and for allowing the pain to define my life.

But as I reflected, I saw how unfair I had been to myself. The little girl I once was didn't deserve blame—she deserved protection. And the woman I had become didn't deserve to carry the guilt of someone else's actions. Giving myself grace meant acknowledging my pain without letting it define me. It meant understanding that healing wasn't about forgetting—it was about accepting that I had done the best I could with what I had.

My acts of care for Edward—bringing him meals, sitting by his bedside, consulting with doctors, traveling long hours to ensure he wasn't alone—became proof of my own growth. In the past, even thinking about him filled me with rage. But now, I saw these gestures not as obligations, but as choices. By opening my heart, I wasn't excusing his actions—I was reclaiming my power. Forgiveness, for me, was less about him and more about stepping into a version of myself no longer shackled by bitterness.

That didn't mean I welcomed him back into my life. Forgiveness was never about reconciliation, restoring a relationship, or seeking his approval. I had no desire to be best friends with Edward, nor did I need his acknowledgment to heal. He was not given access to the beautiful parts of my life that I built despite his betrayal. Chantell and my nieces didn't visit or call him, and he never met my amazing grandchildren, Bryce and Brooklyn. My healing was not tied to his presence or absence but to my decision to release the resentment that had once controlled me.

Letting go wasn't about forgetting—it was about loosening the grip of the past so I could move forward. I chose forgiveness not for him, but for myself—to reclaim my peace, my strength, and the life that pain had overshadowed for too long. It was about setting boundaries, both with Edward and within myself, that allowed me to heal. The openness I once feared became a source of strength. Facing the person who hurt me took courage. But even greater courage was required to forgive—not for his sake, but for mine.

I came to see forgiveness as an act of self-love. Each time I chose it, I was prioritizing my peace and well-being over bitterness. There were still days when anger resurfaced, when memories felt raw and sharp. But there were also days when I felt lighter, unburdened by the past. Forgiveness was not a one-time decision; it was an ongoing commitment to my own healing and growth. With each step forward, I became more attuned to the power I held over my own future.

Rebuilding trust became another essential part of forgiveness. It wasn't about blindly granting others access to my heart; it was about discerning who deserved that access and setting boundaries to protect myself. Trust had to begin within—I had to believe in my own instincts again, to have faith that I could create a life defined by hope rather than fear. As my trust in myself grew, I could extend that trust to those who had proven themselves safe and supportive, rebuilding relationships on a foundation of mutual respect.

Gratitude became a surprising ally in my journey. It didn't erase the pain, but it balanced my perspective. Every choice to forgive—whether it was Edward, myself, or life for its challenges—revealed reasons to be grateful. Grateful for the lessons I had learned, for the strength I had gained, and for the opportunity to start anew. Gratitude reminded me that even in the darkest moments, light could still be found. And with that light came the realization that my story was not just one of pain, but of triumph.

Perhaps the greatest insight forgiveness taught me was the power of love—for myself, for others, and for life. Each act of forgiveness became an act of love, a declaration that I would not let pain dictate my capacity for joy. It was a commitment to living fully and authentically, unshackled by the weight of what had been. I finally understood that neither healing nor forgiveness was about the past—they were about my future.

The suffering I carried had influenced me, but it did not have to define or control me. By forgiving Edward, I reclaimed my story. By forgiving myself, I reclaimed my power. And in doing so, I gave myself the freedom to move forward, no longer bound by wounds inflicted long ago.

Enright and Fitzgibbons (2000) state that people, upon rationally determining that they have been unfairly treated, forgive when they willfully abandon resentment and related responses (to which they have a right), and endeavor to respond to the wrongdoer based on the moral principle of beneficence. This includes compassion, unconditional worth, generosity, and moral love.

Many speak of forgiveness as an important virtue but fail to grasp that it is not about passively waiting for time to heal wounds. Time alone does not heal—healing requires an intentional decision to make space for it in one's heart. It is a choice to replace resentment with compassion, not for the sake of the wrongdoer, but for oneself. True forgiveness is not about denying pain but transforming it into strength. It is about embracing life with an open heart, even after profound hurt. It is a testament to the resilience of the human spirit and the boundless capacity for love and renewal.

CHAPTER XII

The Psychology of Letting Go: Strength and Clarity

Cast all your anxiety on Him because He cares for you.

~ 1 Peter 5:7 (NIV)

Opening my heart to release the anger I had carried was one of the most difficult yet transformative choices I ever made. My focus wasn't on condoning Edward's actions but on creating space for peace—for both of us—in his final days. I knew the weight of his guilt, and I felt a deep conviction to lighten that burden, to help him find some measure of peace as he approached the end of his life.

Seeing his humanity—his regrets, his suffering—did not erase what he had done, but it allowed me to approach him with compassion. This compassion was not just for him; it was also for myself, a recognition that my heart deserved the peace that forgiveness could bring. Holding onto pain would have only continued the cycle of hurt, keeping me tethered to a past I no longer wished to live in. Studies on forgiveness suggest that letting go of resentment can contribute to emotional well-being and reduce psychological distress (Worthington & Scherer, 2004).

My decision to let go of feelings of resentment was not without its challenges. Facing my pain required fortitude and openness. Suppressing my emotions might have felt easier in the short term, but true healing demanded that I confront them head-on. According to research on trauma recovery, acknowledging emotions rather than suppressing them is crucial for growth (Tedeschi & Calhoun, 2004). I had to accept that the past could not be changed and that my power lay in how I chose to respond. My response was not an act of weakness but one of courage. While anger had once been my armor, I recognized that true empowerment lay in my ability to reshape my narrative, not remain trapped within it.

Understanding the significance of my decision required clarity. I needed to define what letting go meant to me in this context. Moving forward in my life was a deliberate choice to no longer let Edward's abuse define my emotional state or dictate the terms of my healing. This clarity allowed me to separate the person from the pain, enabling me to see Edward not just as the perpetrator of harm but also as a human being wrestling with his own remorse. Research suggests that reframing experiences can reduce emotional distress and foster psychological well-being (Neff, 2011). This shift in perspective softened my anger and allowed me to stay by his side, not out of obligation but as a personal decision to reclaim my emotional space.

Empathy became a cornerstone of my decision. This choice required intentionality—it was not a passive act but a deliberate decision to embrace compassion over resentment, guided by my faith and values. I had to confront the layers of my own pain, understanding how anger, once a shield of protection, had become a heavy chain binding me to the past. Letting go had nothing to do with justifying his behavior; it was about freeing myself and reclaiming the peace I needed to embrace the future. Psychological studies indicate that practicing self-compassion can decrease anxiety and increase emotional resilience (Neff & Germer, 2013). In granting Edward forgiveness, I was also granting myself permission to move forward unburdened.

Creativity became an outlet for processing my emotions. Journaling allowed me to explore my feelings in a nonjudgmental way, uncovering insights that helped me make sense of my experience. Writing became a tool for healing, a way to document my growth and articulate the lessons I was learning. Expressive writing has been shown to improve mental and physical health by reducing stress and processing traumatic experiences (Pennebaker, 1997). Each journal entry reminded me that pain, though deeply felt, was also a source of transformation and renewal. I began to see how the act of putting words to my emotions allowed me to reclaim my voice—one that had been silenced for too long.

Spirituality also played a vital role in this journey. Through prayer and reflection, I found guidance and comfort, a sense that I was not alone in this difficult process. My faith reminded me that forgiveness was not just an act of letting go but also an act of grace, an alignment with the principles of love and compassion that I hold dear. Research supports that spirituality and faith can be protective factors in coping with trauma, offering a sense of meaning and emotional resilience (Pargament, 2001). This spiritual connection gave me the strength to follow through with my decision, even when it felt overwhelming. My prayers became a dialogue with something greater than myself, helping me to trust that healing was possible, even when the pain felt insurmountable.

The process of letting go required patience. Some days, I felt a sense of peace, a lightness that I hadn't known before. Other days, I struggled with doubt, wondering if I had made the right choice. The emotional weight of Edward's actions did not simply disappear overnight; rather, it dissipated in waves, each moment of understanding replacing a fragment of resentment. Psychological studies suggest that forgiveness is a gradual process, often requiring repeated efforts to mentally and emotionally disengage from past harm (McCullough, Pargament, & Thoresen, 2000). It became clear to me that healing wasn't a single event but a continuous unfolding, an ongoing commitment to myself.

Through this process, I learned the importance of redefining power. For so long, I had subconsciously allowed Edward's actions to hold sway over my sense of self. Reclaiming my power meant deciding that his actions would no longer dictate my narrative. This realization allowed me to take control of my story, shifting from a place of pain to one of purpose. Psychological resilience is often linked to the ability to reinterpret life experiences in ways that foster growth and adaptability (Bonanno, 2004). By embracing this understanding, I saw that my future would not be shaped by the pain he caused but by the strength and clarity I found within myself.

As I spent time with Edward during his final days, I could see the toll that guilt and shame had taken on him. His remorse was palpable, and I knew that carrying those heavy emotions would only add to his suffering. Studies indicate that unresolved guilt can contribute to emotional distress and deteriorate mental health (Tangney, Stuewig, & Mashek, 2007). I hoped to lighten his load, to give him the space to find his own peace before it was too late. In doing so, I also began to feel a sense of relief, as though releasing my anger was simultaneously lifting a burden I had carried for decades.

Forgiveness does not mean forgetting, nor does it mean that the past ceases to matter. Instead, it is a conscious choice to refuse to be defined by wounds inflicted by another. The act of letting go became an assertion of my own worth, a decision to prioritize my emotional and mental well-being. Studies on post-traumatic growth suggest that those who engage in meaning-making after trauma report greater psychological strength and purpose (Joseph & Linley, 2005). I chose to step forward, not because Edward deserved my forgiveness, but because I deserve peace.

In the end, I understood that healing is a deeply personal evolution. By letting go of my anger and embracing compassion, I was able to honor his humanity and my own. This transformation redefined my relationship with pain, with time, and with myself. The final lesson in this season of my life was that true strength lies in our ability to embrace love, extend grace, and move forward with a heart unburdened by the past.

*"Do not judge me by my success,
judge me by how many times I fell down
and got back up again."*

—Nelson Mandela

CHAPTER XIII

Releasing the Shame: Embracing Resilience

Shame dies when stories are told in safe places.

~ Ann Voskamp

S hame held me captive for years. It wasn't just the fear of being judged or disbelieved—it was the insidious belief that what happened to me defined my worth. That lie took root early, convincing me that I was damaged, that I carried an invisible mark only I could see but one that shaped every aspect of my identity. Shame was not just an emotion; it became a lens through which I viewed myself and my place in the world. It altered the way I saw relationships, trust, and my own value.

It whispered that trust was dangerous, that if people truly knew my story, they would turn away. Even those closest to me felt distant because I feared their rejection. I longed for connection but remained trapped behind walls of my own making, convinced that love was conditional, that vulnerability would only expose me to more hurt. In my isolation, I mistook self-protection for safety, unaware that I was reinforcing my own loneliness.

For women, shame carries an even heavier weight because society often places responsibility on us—on what we wear, where we go, and how cautious we are. When harm happens, the unspoken message lingers: *You should have prevented this.* I absorbed that narrative and turned it inward, questioning whether my silence as a child made me complicit. That misplaced guilt clung to me for years, making me feel powerless and small.

But the truth was that shame never belonged to me. It belonged to the one who inflicted the harm. What happened was not a reflection of who I was, but a choice made by someone else. That realization loosened its grip, allowing me to reclaim the truth: I had been wronged, but I was never to blame.

For decades, I carried my pain in silence, hoping that if I ignored it long enough, it would disappear. But instead, it festered beneath the surface, influencing my choices and clouding my self-worth. I didn't believe I deserved happiness, love, or success. I lived in fear that others would one day see what I had convinced myself was true—that I was broken beyond repair.

That belief seeped into every area of my life, making me question whether I was worthy of peace or healing. I became skilled at suppressing my emotions, shoving them so deep that they wouldn't interfere with my life. But true healing required more than avoidance; it demanded that I confront the pain I had spent years trying to escape. When I began visiting Edward in the hospital, I had to allow myself to feel—anger, sadness, confusion, grief—so that I could finally begin to release them. And as I did, I felt something I hadn't in a long time: *relief.*

I started to embrace the process of reclaiming my self-worth and reconnecting with the parts of me that had been buried under shame. I rediscovered what brought me joy, the dreams I had set aside, the relationships I had distanced myself from out of fear. Every small step I took toward healing was a step back to myself. It wasn't about erasing the past but about refusing to let it dictate my future.

One of the most challenging yet necessary steps was learning to set boundaries. For too long, I allowed guilt to keep me from asserting my needs. I felt like saying no was selfish, that prioritizing my well-being meant shutting others out. But I came to realize that boundaries weren't about exclusion—they were about protection. Learning to say no without explanation was empowering. I was no longer obligated to justify my right to peace.

Grieving was another crucial step in my healing. Abuse had taken things from me—my sense of security, my innocence, and my ability to trust. Mourning those losses was painful, but it was also necessary. Acknowledging that pain was not a sign of weakness; it was a declaration that what I endured mattered. That *I* mattered.

Letting go of self-blame was perhaps the hardest step of all. For years, I carried guilt that never belonged to me. But through deep reflection, I began to see that children are never responsible for protecting themselves from harm—that responsibility lies with the adults around them. Releasing myself from the false belief that I should have done something differently was an act of self-liberation. I had spent so much time asking myself, *Why didn't I fight harder? Why didn't I tell sooner?* But those were the wrong questions. The real question was: *Why did I ever believe it was my burden to carry?*

Mindfulness helped me stay anchored in the present. Shame often dragged me back into the past, replaying painful memories and reinforcing the lies I had believed for so long. Mindfulness broke that cycle, allowing me to be present in the life I was creating rather than being trapped in the one I had survived. I realized that healing wasn't about forgetting—it was about reclaiming my life.

It took courage to confront my past, but even greater courage to choose grace over bitterness. Each small victory—setting a boundary, sharing my truth, or choosing to care for myself—was proof that I was no longer trapped by shame. As I moved from shame to healing, I found purpose in my experiences. I realized that sharing my story could bring hope to others still trapped in silence.

My voice, once silenced by shame, became a source of empowerment. Self-compassion became the antidote to my shame. For the first time, I began to see myself not through the lens of my trauma, but through the lens of strength. Yes, I had endured something painful—but I had *survived*. That alone was proof of my resilience.

Slowly, I rebuilt my self-worth. I stopped defining myself by what had been done to me and started defining myself by how I chose to rise. The journey from shame to healing has not been easy. There were setbacks, doubts, and moments when I wanted to retreat into old patterns. But with each step forward, I reminded myself that I was not reclaiming just my story—I was reclaiming *myself*.

Therapy was a turning point in my journey. Speaking my truth felt terrifying at first. But as I sat in that space and allowed myself to say the words I had never spoken aloud, I realized I no longer had to carry my pain alone. I learned that my responses—whether self-doubt, fear, or even anger—were normal reactions to trauma. That realization freed me. Instead of punishing myself for struggling, I began offering myself kindness. The same compassion I so readily gave to others, I began to extend to myself.

That shift changed everything. I no longer saw healing as an obligation or something I needed to "fix" about myself—I saw it as an act of love. A commitment to honoring my worth, my strength, my survival. Actively healing allowed me to reclaim my voice, my worth, and my future. But no matter how much progress I made, there were still pieces of my past that lingered in the shadows—unresolved, unspoken, and waiting to be confronted. Some wounds do not simply fade with time; they resurface in unexpected moments, reminding us that true healing requires more than just moving forward—it requires facing what we once tried to forget.

*"It is through unconditional love
that liberation becomes inevitable."*

- Alexander Lopez

CHAPTER XIV:

When Love Becomes Liberation

> *There is no fear in love. But perfect love drives out fear, because fear has to do with punishment.*
>
> ~ 1 John 4:18 (NIV)

As an adult, I found it effortless to navigate my life as if Edward had never been a part of it. He had been a ghost in my mind—a presence I refused to acknowledge, a chapter of my past that I had sealed shut. But he was there. I would pass him as he rode his bike through the streets of Jacksonville, catching only glimpses of him as I drove into town to visit my family.

On occasion, I did encounter him face to face. When he showed up uninvited to a Mother's Day dinner at my childhood home, I ignored him. He was also there when my sister Beverly passed away, standing in the background at her wake, as though he were just another mourner. I never allowed myself to react to him. I had convinced myself that he did not matter, that his existence had no bearing on mine—but deep down, I knew that was a lie.

The truth was, I had spent years suppressing the weight of what he had done. To acknowledge him meant acknowledging the pain, and that was something I had spent a lifetime avoiding. I had trained myself to be indifferent to his presence, to feel nothing. It was a kind of survival mechanism, a way to maintain control over emotions that threatened to consume me. But when Edward became ill, something inside me shifted. Despite all the years of silence and avoidance, I chose to be there. Caring for him forced me to confront what I had spent decades burying. It was no longer possible to ignore his existence, and in that realization, I discovered something unexpected: liberation.

At first, I did not know what to make of the emotions that surfaced. As I tended to his needs, I felt small flickers of love rising within me—strange and unfamiliar, as if they had been dormant for years. I was unsure if the love I felt was for him as my brother or for him as a fellow human being in pain. Did I love him because we shared blood, or did I simply recognize his suffering in a way that transcended history? I did not know the answer, and maybe it did not matter. What mattered was that I no longer had to suppress or compartmentalize my thoughts and emotions. I could acknowledge both the pain he had caused and the love that still managed to surface. And in that process, I felt a weight begin to lift.

For so long, I had carried the burden of unresolved pain. Trauma, when left unchecked, becomes a prison—one that traps not only the body but also the mind and spirit (Herman, 1997). I had built walls around my emotions, believing that if I could control what I allowed myself to feel, I could prevent myself from being hurt again. But those walls had not protected me; they had only confined me. Holding onto pain had not given me power—it had only reinforced my suffering. And so, in choosing to show up for Edward, in choosing love even when it was undeserved, I released myself.

Forgiveness is often misunderstood. It is not about condoning harm, nor is it about pretending that the past does not exist. Instead, it is about releasing the grip that pain has on our lives (Enright & Fitzgibbons, 2000). In choosing to care for Edward, I was not erasing history. I was not dismissing the trauma or rewriting the narrative of what he had done to me. I was simply refusing to let that trauma dictate the rest of my life. By acknowledging my pain instead of burying it, I reclaimed the power that had been taken from me. That was the real act of liberation.

It was difficult to explain this to those around me. But what they did not realize was that walking away would not have freed me—it would have only reinforced the compartmentalization that had dictated my emotional life for years. Choosing to stay, choosing to care, was not about him. It was about me.

Pain thrives in secrecy. When we refuse to acknowledge it, when we push it down and lock it away, it festers. It grows in the silence, shaping our decisions, our relationships, our sense of self (van der Kolk, 2014). I had spent too many years letting my pain dictate the way I moved through the world. I refused to let it continue. Caring for Edward was my way of stepping out of the silence. It was my way of reclaiming my narrative—not as a victim, not as someone controlled by past trauma, but as someone who had the strength to face it head-on.

The act of releasing pain is transformative. Studies show that those who engage in emotional processing *and* forgiveness practices experience reduced anxiety, lower stress levels, and an increased sense of purpose (Worthington & Scherer, 2004). As I leaned into the process of care, I began to understand why love—true, unburdened love—is so powerful. Love does not erase the past, but it allows for a new kind of future. It does not mean forgetting, but it does mean choosing to move forward with peace. In showing love to Edward, I was showing love to myself.

This experience taught me that love, when given without conditions, can be one of the most profound forms of liberation. It is not about the person receiving it—it is about the person giving it. Love allowed me to step outside of the rigid emotional structure I had built for myself. It softened the edges of my pain, allowing me to breathe again. It gave me permission to exist outside of trauma, to see myself as more than just what had happened to me. Love did not change Edward, but it changed me.

Choosing love over resentment is a radical act. It is a form of resistance against the pain that seeks to keep us locked in place. Trauma tells us that we are unworthy, that we are damaged, that we are incapable of feeling whole again. Love dismantles that lie. Love whispers that healing is possible, that even in the darkest places, there is still light. By choosing love, I chose myself. I chose freedom.

I do not regret showing up for Edward. The process was not easy, and it did not come without struggle. But in the end, it was the right decision—for me. It allowed me to move forward in a way that I never thought possible. Letting go of resentment freed me, but true liberation required something more—grace. Love had opened the door to healing, but faith was what carried me through it. It taught me that healing was not just about making peace with the past, but about extending compassion, even to those whose choices had shaped my pain. And so, just as I had found the strength to care for Edward, I began to examine the wounds left by others in my life, starting with my parents."

CHAPTER XV

A Bridge to Grace

> *My grace is sufficient for you,*
> *for my power is made perfect*
> *in weakness."*
>
> ~ 2 Corinthians 12:9 (NIV)

Faith has an extraordinary way of opening our hearts to grace, even when the pain feels insurmountable. It allows us to confront the deepest wounds while uncovering the courage to release pain and bitterness. For me, faith was more than a bridge—it was a lifeline, connecting my pain to the healing I desperately needed.

One of the most eye-opening realizations on this journey was the importance of giving grace. Extending grace required me to look beyond the surface of hurt and see the humanity in those who had unintentionally contributed to my pain. This process began with my parents. As an adult, I came to realize that both my parents had suffered profound childhood trauma of their own.

Their lives were marked by discrimination, poverty, parental abandonment, and the absence of support systems that could have guided them through their struggles. These challenges left them with their own wounds, and, as a result, gaps in their parenting emerged. Their intentions were never to harm us. They believed their actions were protective, though their methods were shaped by their limited tools and experiences.

My mother left the home with the confidence that my dad would take care of our needs in ways that she could not due to her financial situation. My father, while navigating the pain of my mother's departure, took on the responsibility of providing for us. He built a home and made sure we had what we needed—meals on the table, clothes on our backs, and everything essential for school and extracurricular activities. Though he rarely said the words, his love was evident in the way he showed up for us. His actions spoke volumes. Love is not always demonstrated in the ways we expect, but it can be found in the quiet sacrifices made on our behalf.

As I began to understand my parents more fully, I realized that their shortcomings were not a result of a lack of love but of limited resources—emotional, psychological, and spiritual. Their struggles didn't excuse the negative impacts, but they provided context. Their parenting, flawed as it was, came from a place of love and a desire to shield us in the only ways they knew how. Their choices, shaped by their own trauma, had left scars, but they had also instilled perseverance. By choosing to extend grace and forgiveness, I was breaking a chain that could have easily continued into future generations. This realization gave me hope and a sense of purpose.

This understanding didn't come easily. Subconsciously, I had carried a lingering sense of guilt, rooted in the belief that if my parents had been more emotionally present, perhaps the abuse I experienced might have been prevented. While I never directly blamed them, the loneliness I felt during crucial moments in my life was something I couldn't ignore. Maturity, however, helped me reframe this perspective. Instead of seeing them as negligent, I began to see them as imperfect individuals doing their best under difficult circumstances.

As children, we rarely understand the various components of our parents' lives. We see them as our caregivers, our protectors, and sometimes even as invincible figures. It's only later, often through our own life experiences, that we begin to uncover the depth of their struggles and the ways those hardships influenced their choices. If I had known as a child the full extent of my parents' pain, I might have found it easier to extend grace. As an adult and a mother, I believe that, despite their shortcomings, they truly had my best interests at heart.

Grace allowed me to see beyond my parents' actions and recognize the pain they carried. Their struggles with domestic violence and other family issues were not isolated events but part of a broader cycle of generational trauma. Faith helped me understand that their limitations were not reflections of their love for me. This understanding didn't diminish the hurt I experienced, but it gave me the ability to extend kindness to them.

One of the lessons I learned was that my parents were not only parents—they were people. They had dreams, fears, and burdens of their own, many of which I could never entirely comprehend. Once I began to see them through this lens, it was easier to let go of the subtle resentment I had carried for so long. I realized that grace is not about erasing pain but about making room for appreciation and kindness. Granting grace to my parents allowed me to hold space for their humanity without dismissing my own experiences. I could honor my story without being imprisoned by it.

One of the greatest gifts I received from my parents was tenacity. They believed in the power of education and pushed me to go to college, to be independent and self-sufficient. It wasn't until adulthood that I fully understood the complexities of their struggles. The sacrifices they made, the hardships they endured, and even the decisions I once resented all became clearer with time. Understanding this softened the sharp edges of my frustration. I am thankful for them both.

Granting grace to others often begins with compassion, and faith was the key that unlocked that awareness. Through prayer and reflection, I came to see that holding onto bitterness toward my parents didn't change the past—it only kept me bound to it. Faith reminded me that releasing anger was not about excusing what had happened but about lifting myself from its hold.

Grace and accountability are not mutually exclusive. Recognizing my parents' challenges and the gaps in their parenting didn't mean overlooking the effects those gaps had on my life. Instead, it required me to accept both realities: that they were human individuals who loved me and that their missteps had tangible consequences. Finding this balance became a crucial part of my healing process.

One of the scriptures that guided me was Ephesians 4:32: "Be kind and compassionate to one another, forgiving each other, just as in Christ God forgave you." This verse reminded me that forgiveness is an act of grace, modeled by God Himself. If God could extend grace to me in my imperfections, then I could offer it to others, including my parents. Because I loved them both deeply, it felt natural.

Grace wasn't just for others; it was also for myself. I had carried guilt for years—for blaming my parents and for struggling to heal. My emotions, no matter how complex, were valid. Releasing the past wasn't about perfection; it was about entrusting my pain to God and allowing Him to shape it into something meaningful.

Faith taught me that true grace is restorative. It doesn't erase accountability but rather seeks to heal the wounds left behind. I prayed for God's help in releasing the negative feelings and thoughts I held toward my parents, and over time, I began to see myself as He sees me—valued, loved, and deserving of healing. His compassion reminded me that my story, though marked by pain, held the possibility of renewal and hope.

Grace became my foundation, guiding me away from anger and blame toward understanding and kindness. Even in moments of brokenness, we remain unconditionally loved and capable of restoration. As grace led me toward healing, the lasting effects of trauma did not simply fade away. The wounds of childhood, though covered by faith and resilience, continued to shape my body, mind, and emotions in ways I could not always control. Healing required more than just spiritual renewal—it demanded that I confront the deep, lingering impact of my past.

As I began to understand how trauma had affected me, I also realized the importance of sharing this awareness with others. If I could shed light on the hidden scars so many survivors carry, perhaps I could help break the cycle of silence and create space for others to begin their own healing.

"Trauma changes you.

Healing is about creating a new version of yourself,

the one that is stronger, wiser,

and more compassionate."

– Michele Rosenthal

CHAPTER XVI

Rewriting the Narrative: Turning Trauma into Testimony

Your past is just a story.
And once you realize this,
it has no power over you.

~ Chuck Palahniuk

T rauma has a way of embedding itself into the fabric of a person's life, often persisting far beyond the original event. For individuals who have endured significant childhood trauma, like I have, the psychological and physiological effects can linger well into adulthood. Depression and anxiety are common struggles, emerging as the mind attempts to process what was never meant to be endured. The body's response to trauma can lead to chronic stress, digestive issues, autoimmune disorders, and other health complications that stem from prolonged exposure to fear and distress.

Many individuals turn to substance abuse to numb the emotional pain, seeking relief in ways that only offer temporary escape. Unresolved trauma can also manifest in unhealthy relationships, difficulties with trust, and an inability to set boundaries. The scars of trauma are not always visible, but their impact runs deep, molding how we see ourselves and how we interact with the world. I, too, have carried these scars.

The echoes of my past haunted my thoughts, influencing my self-worth and my ability to fully embrace life. But one day, I realized that although I could not change my past, I had the power to change how I respond to it. Trauma does not have to be a life sentence—it does not have to dictate the rest of our lives. I am rewriting my narrative, to shift from being a survivor of trauma to someone who uses her experience as a testimony of resilience.

I share my experiences because I have found healing and believe it is possible for others who have walked a similar path. Expressing our truths allows us to reclaim our voices, take ownership of our past, and find purpose in our struggles. I knew that if I remained silent, I would continue giving my trauma more power than it deserved.

There is something deeply restorative about breaking the silence that once held me captive. At first, I feared judgment, misunderstanding, and rejection. But as I spoke to others, I realized my words resonated with women and men who had endured similar experiences. I was not alone in my pain, and neither were they. There is strength in shared under-standing—when we hear someone else articulate the struggles we have faced, it affirms our emotions and reminds us that healing is possible.

Each time I express my truth; I take another step toward reclaiming my strength. Through this process, I have come to recognize that my trauma does not define me; it is merely a chapter in my journey, not the whole story. My voice is no longer bound by shame or secrecy. Instead, it has become a tool of empowerment, offering hope to those still search-ing for their own path to healing. Holding onto resentment stunts emo-tional healing, keeping individuals trapped in a cycle of pain and anger.

By forgiving—not just Edward, but also myself for the years I spent carrying the burden—I have opened the door to a deeper transformation.

The impact of testimony goes beyond personal healing—it serves as an educational tool, helping society understand the realities of trauma and the complexities of recovery. Many people who have never experienced abuse or deep trauma struggle to grasp its long-term effects. By discussing my journey, I have been able to shed light on the challenges survivors face and the resilience it takes to overcome them.

Awareness leads to empathy, and empathy leads to action. If my story can inspire even one person to become more compassionate, to offer support to a survivor, or to challenge societal stigmas, then every painful moment I have endured has not been in vain. Testimony is a catalyst for change. When survivors speak out, they challenge the cultural norms that perpetuate silence and stigma. Too often, trauma is buried beneath shame, hidden behind closed doors, and ignored by those who would rather not acknowledge its existence. But when we refuse to stay silent, we demand accountability. We call for justice. We encourage others to act—not just in their personal lives, but in their communities, their institutions, and their policies. There is power in speaking truth to pain. There is power in saying, *I will not be silent about what happened to me, and I will not allow others to suffer in silence either.*

Sharing my testimony has not only been a means of healing for myself, but a way to encourage and uplift others who feel trapped in their silence. When survivors speak their truth, they create space for others to do the same. Too many people suffer in isolation, believing that their pain is theirs alone to bear. But when someone steps forward and says, *I have been there, and I survived,* it offers a beacon of hope. It tells others that healing is possible, that life after trauma can still be full of joy, love, and purpose. Each time I share my story; I am reminded that vulnerability is not weakness—it is the bridge that connects us to others who need to hear that they are not alone.

The concept of post-traumatic growth has been instrumental in my journey toward healing. According to Tedeschi & Calhoun (2004), post-traumatic growth occurs when an individual experiences positive psychological change because of struggling with adversity. This growth manifests in several key areas: appreciation of life, deepened relationships with others, new possibilities, personal strength, spiritual growth, and forgiveness.

Through my growth, I have come to recognize my own strength in ways I never imagined. It takes courage to face the darkest parts of our past, to confront pain that has been buried for years. But I have done that work, and I continue to do it every day. I have survived, and beyond that, I have thrived. I no longer see myself as weak or broken—I see myself as strong, empowered, and capable of building a future that is not defined by my trauma. This shift in perspective has been life-changing; I am no longer a prisoner of my past. Instead, I am the author of my story.

Healing is about taking what was meant to break us and using it to build something meaningful. I have turned my pain into purpose, and in doing so, I have found the deepest form of healing. My story is not just one of survival, but of transformation. By choosing to rewrite my narrative, I have discovered that I am more than what happened to me—I am what I choose to become.

Healing does not happen in isolation—it is deeply intertwined with the generations that came before us. Pain is often inherited, passed down in ways we may not recognize until we start to unravel our own wounds. To truly heal, I had to look beyond my own experiences and confront the patterns of trauma that shaped my family long before I was born.

CHAPTER XVII

Intergenerational Trauma and Adverse Childhood Experiences

> *The ghosts of our ancestors are present in the ways we live, love, and heal. Breaking cycles is an act of courage.*
>
> ~ Dr. Thelma Bryant

Some wounds run deeper than a single lifetime. Pain and hardship do not always start with us—they often begin long before we take our first breath, passed down like an unspoken inheritance. Trauma settles into our families, shaping how we love, how we cope, and how we raise the next generation (Yehuda & Lehrner, 2018).

For a long time, I didn't understand why my childhood felt like a storm I couldn't escape. Why my father was distant. Why my mother chose to move 3,000 miles away from North Carolina to California instead of settling in a nearby state where she could have seen us more often and remained a more present figure in our lives. She accepted that decision, perhaps believing it was what she needed for her own survival or maybe convinced that the distance would offer a fresh start, free from the adversities of her past. But as I started to piece together their histories, I began to see the patterns—the echoes of pain carried forward from generation to generation.

Adverse Childhood Experiences (ACEs) refer to the difficult and traumatic events that occur in childhood—such as abuse, neglect, parental separation, violence, or substance abuse in the home. The ACE Study (Appendix A) was developed in the 1990s by Dr. Vincent Felitti and Dr. Robert Anda at Kaiser Permanente and the Centers for Disease Control and Prevention (Felitti et al., 1998). What started as an obesity study unexpectedly uncovered deep-rooted connections between childhood trauma and long-term health risks.

When Felitti and his team examined the early life experiences of patients, they found a staggering pattern—people who had endured multiple forms of trauma in childhood were significantly more likely to suffer from chronic diseases, mental health disorders, and early mortality. The ACE Study revolutionized the way we understand trauma, linking childhood adversity to lifelong health consequences in ways that had never been formally studied before.

The study identified ten categories of ACEs, including physical, emotional, and sexual abuse, neglect, household substance abuse, domestic violence, and parental incarceration (Felitti et al., 1998). The research found that individuals with four or more ACEs were at a significantly higher risk of developing heart disease, depression, substance abuse, and other serious health issues (Centers for Disease Control and Prevention [CDC], 2021).

Our parents likely had high ACE scores, long before they had children of their own, and the impact of their unresolved trauma shaped our upbringing in ways we did not understand at the time. My father lost his mother as a child, and instead of finding comfort in his father, he was abandoned. Left with no parents to love or guide him, he was raised by his paternal grandmother. She provided him and his siblings with a home, but nothing could replace the deep loss and emotional deprivation he experienced. He grew up knowing poverty, hardship, and what it felt like to be unwanted.

Later in life, he reconnected with his father, but by then, the damage was already done. Research has found that children who experience early parental loss or abandonment are more likely to develop attachment issues, self-doubt, and emotional dysregulation in adulthood (Masten & Barnes, 2018). I understand why my father was so focused on making sure our physical needs were met—food on the table, a roof over our heads—but why he struggled to provide the emotional care we needed. He had never been given that himself.

My mother's childhood was also shaped by familial instability and trauma. Her grandmother had abandoned her mother and uncle when they were children, leaving them to be raised by other family members. That loss shaped the way my grandmother raised my mother, passing down a sense of emotional distance, a survival mindset that left little room for softness. But perhaps the most painful wound in my mother's past was the fact that her father was incarcerated for murdering her stepmother.

The absence of a parent due to incarceration is one of the strongest risk factors for trauma and later-life instability, as children in these circumstances are more likely to face financial hardships, emotional neglect, and social difficulties (Turney & Haskins, 2014). When I think about the hardships both of my parents endured, I no longer see them as just "flawed parents"—I see two people who were doing the best they could with the tools they had. And those tools had been shaped by generations of hardship.

The ACE Study not only highlighted the risks associated with childhood trauma but also revealed the intergenerational impact of parental ACEs. Research has shown that parents who experience high ACE scores are more likely to raise children who also experience high ACEs—not because they don't love their children, but because unhealed trauma finds a way to resurface (Shonkoff et al., 2012). Parents who grew up in emotionally neglectful environments often struggle to provide emotional support for their children.

Parents who endured violence, instability, or addiction may unintentionally recreate those cycles, even when they desperately want to do better. My father's drinking, my mother's absence, the dysfunction, and the emotional disconnection—it all made sense when I looked at the bigger picture. And that bigger picture made me realize that the pain I experienced as a child was not just my own. It was part of something much larger.

My siblings and I each have a score of four or higher, which means we were statistically set up for struggle before we even had a chance to understand the world. But what hit me even harder was realizing that this didn't start with us. Understanding intergenerational trauma helped me make sense of why certain patterns repeated in my family. Why love sometimes felt distant. Why survival seemed more important than emotional connection.

Trauma is not just something that happens to an individual—it becomes embedded in families, communities, and even biological responses (Yehuda & Lehrner, 2018). Studies have shown that the stress response system of children who grow up in chaotic or abusive environments becomes overactive, making them more likely to experience chronic stress, anxiety, and depression later in life (van der Kolk, 2014). Considering my family's history, I could see how trauma shaped not just my parents, but also my grandparents, and likely their parents before them.

But here's the truth I've come to understand; trauma does not have to be a life sentence. Cycles can be broken. Pain can stop with us. The fact that trauma runs in my family does not mean that I am doomed to pass it on to the next generation. I have the power to choose a different path. Healing is a choice, and though it is not an easy one, it is a necessary one.

However, I can't help but wish I had possessed this understanding when I was raising my own daughter. I did the best I could with what I knew at the time, but I see the missed opportunities to nurture her emotional well-being in ways I had never been taught myself.

Today, I have the knowledge and insight to do things differently with my grandchildren, ensuring they grow up in an environment of transparency, emotional safety, and unconditional love. While I can't rewrite the past, I can move forward with intention, ensuring that the legacy I leave is one of healing, not hurt.

Breaking the cycle of trauma is not just a personal commitment—it is a societal necessity. The prevalence of sexual harm within families is an undeniable truth, one that too many survivors, including myself, have had to endure alone. Understanding the scope of this issue is essential in ensuring that future generations do not suffer the same fate.

"Tell the story of the mountain you climbed.

Your words could become a page

in someone else's survival guide."

— Morgan Harper Nichols

CHAPTER XVIII

The Silent Betrayal: Unveiling the Reality of Sibling Sexual Abuse

*Nothing strengthens authority
so much as silence."*

~ Leonardo da Vinci

The Centers for Disease Control and Prevention (CDC) reports that one in four girls and one in thirteen boys will experience some form of sexual harm before the age of eighteen, with 90% of the perpetrators being family friends or relatives. These statistics are not just numbers; they represent the devastating reality that, for many children, the danger comes from those closest to them—the very people entrusted with their care and protection. This betrayal does not just cause immediate harm; it reshapes the survivor's understanding of safety, trust, and self-worth, leaving wounds that can last a lifetime.

Sexual abuse within families is one of the most difficult topics to discuss, and when the abuser is an older sibling, the layers of complexity and secrecy become even more profound. According to a report by the Centre of Expertise on Child Sexual Abuse (2021), the most common reported pattern of sibling sexual abuse involves an older brother abusing a younger sister. The report also states that when families fail to act, the impact on the victim's life can be exacerbated, compounding the trauma and making healing even more difficult.

Shame, secrecy, and misguided loyalty often prevent survivors from speaking out. In many Black families, there is a deeply ingrained mantra: "What happens in our household stays in our household." This culture of silence can create a protective shield around abusers while leaving victims without support.

As a child, I quickly learned the weight of silence. My father became aware of the abuse when I was ten years old, years after it began, and I accidentally exposed it in front of a family friend. We had a brief, uncomfortable conversation—uncomfortable not only because of the topic, but because it was clear my father was ill-equipped to handle it. He seemed unsure of what to say, how to comfort me, or even how to acknowledge the depth of what I had shared. His discomfort was palpable, not rooted in indifference, but in a lack of emotional tools and perhaps even his own unresolved pain. I suspect he believed that removing Edward from the home would resolve the issue, and indeed, shortly after our conversation, Edward left for a couple of years.

No one asked how I was doing. No one followed up. The silence that followed spoke volumes—it was as if addressing the abuse directly would make it more real, and perhaps my father didn't have the capacity to face that reality. So, we moved forward as if nothing had happened, but I carried the unspoken truth with me. When Edward returned home during my teenage years, the silence remained, and with it, the unspoken reality that nothing had truly been addressed.

But silence does not resolve abuse. It deepens the wound, reinforcing a victim's sense of worthlessness and isolation. For me, that silence became a second betrayal, one that left me wondering whether I mattered enough to be protected. My father's inaction did not mean he approved of what had happened, but his uncertainty and avoidance sent me a message that still lingers: some pains are too heavy to acknowledge.

Complicating the situation further were the unresolved struggles between my parents. My father was carrying his own burdens—he had been left to raise children after my mother left the home. While he provided for our basic needs, his emotional availability was limited. I can't say with certainty whether his silence about the abuse was due to emotional exhaustion, shame, or his own lack of understanding, but what I do know is that he never told my mother. When I attempted to discuss the abuse with her as an adult, I was shocked to discover that she had no idea.

Her response—or lack thereof—deepened my feelings of shame. Instead of engaging in a conversation, offering comfort, or seeking understanding, she refused to discuss it. Her silence was yet another confirmation that what had happened to me was unspeakable, that it was something I should carry alone. I walked away from that conversation feeling even more isolated, reaffirming the toxic belief that my pain was something to be hidden rather than addressed.

This is why parents must foster open conversations with their children about body safety, boundaries, and consent. Too often, children—especially in strict or religious households—are not given the language or the tools to understand inappropriate behavior, let alone report it. If I had been told, explicitly and clearly, that no one had the right to touch me in a way that made me uncomfortable—even a sibling—I may have spoken up sooner.

Parents must be proactive, not reactive, when it comes to protecting their children. Conversations about "safe and appropriate touching" should begin at an early age and continue as children grow. These discussions must go beyond simple warnings about "strangers" and acknowledge that harm often comes from trusted individuals within the home. Teaching children how to assert their boundaries and recognize manipulative behavior is one of the most powerful forms of prevention.

Had my parents created an environment where discussing uncomfortable topics was normalized, I may have found the courage to speak up earlier. Instead, the dysfunction in their marriage, the tensions in our home, and the silence that surrounded difficult conversations created the perfect conditions for the abuse to remain hidden. Their struggles were real, but their unresolved pain had unintended consequences—it left me without the support I desperately needed.

There is also an important power dynamic at play in cases of sibling sexual abuse. Older siblings hold authority in the home, particularly in families where parents are absent or preoccupied. When that power is abused, younger siblings may feel they have no choice but to comply. I was not just Edward's younger sister—I was the child of a fractured home, a girl trying to navigate an unstable emotional landscape. Edward's actions exploited that exposure, and my father's silence further cemented my powerlessness

Intervening in cases of sibling sexual abuse is not just about stopping the abuse—it is about addressing the damage that has already been done. Parents must seek professional intervention, not only for the victim but for the abuser as well. Therapy is essential for both parties to address the underlying issues, prevent recurrence, and break the cycle of trauma.

Ignoring the problem, hoping it will resolve itself, or believing that separation will erase the damage only deepens the long-term consequences.

The shame I carried for years was not just about what Edward did—it was about how the people around me responded, or rather, failed to respond. Healing required me to acknowledge that I had been failed, not just by my abuser, but by the silence that followed. It took me years to understand that their inaction was not a reflection of my worth but of their own limitations.

If I could go back and speak to my younger self, I would tell her that her pain mattered. That she was worthy of protection. That her silence was never proof of complicity—it was proof of the overwhelming power of shame. And I would remind her that she was never alone, even when it felt that way.

Sibling sexual abuse remains one of the most underreported and misunderstood forms of child abuse. But the secrecy surrounding it only enables further harm. By having open, honest, and ongoing conversations, by addressing power imbalances within the home, and by taking swift action when abuse is disclosed, we can prevent future harm and allow survivors to reclaim their voices.

Healing from sibling sexual abuse is not just about overcoming trauma—it is about dismantling the structures that allowed it to happen in the first place. We must replace silence with conversation, shame with empowerment, and secrecy with accountability. Only then can we truly begin to break the cycle. Survivors deserve more than silence. They deserve justice, support, and the freedom to heal without shame.

Yet, healing is not confined to personal reflection—it also requires confronting the emotional, familial, and societal factors that shape a survivor's experience. The weight of trauma does not disappear simply because time has passed; it lingers, influencing relationships, self-perception, and the ability to trust again.

*"The ultimate tragedy
is not the oppression and cruelty
by the bad people
but the silence over that
by the good people."*

— Dr Martin Luther King Jr.

CHAPTER XIX

Silence Is Not Golden

> *Speak up for those who cannot speak*
> *for themselves; ensure justice*
> *for those being crushed.*
>
> ~ Proverbs 31:8 (NLT)

T he shame of sexual abuse leaves invisible marks on its victims—wounds that are deeply felt, even if they cannot be seen. These scars last long beyond the abuse itself, shaping the way survivors view themselves and interact with the world. While physical evidence of abuse may fade, the emotional and psychological aftermath lingers, often in silence. That silence, for many, feels safer than confronting the stigma, judgment, and blame that society so often places on victims.

Even in a time of increasing awareness, a powerful stigma remains. Despite advocacy and education, many survivors feel pressure to keep their pain hidden for fear of being judged, dismissed, or disbelieved. This is not a reflection of their weakness but a testament to the systemic failures that continue to discourage survivors from speaking out. Silence becomes a survival mechanism, reinforced by a world that too often demands proof of suffering before offering compassion.

Survivors of sexual abuse—whether through rape, childhood molestation, or exploitation—are often met with harmful responses. Victim-blaming persists, with questions about their actions, clothing, or choices overshadowing the perpetrator's guilt. For child survivors, blame sometimes shifts to their parents, scrutinizing their vigilance rather than holding the abuser accountable. These reactions deepen the wounds of those who have already endured so much, reinforcing the damaging belief that they are responsible for what happened to them.

For children who experience sexual abuse, the trauma can shape their entire worldview. Many adult survivors trace struggles with intimacy, self-worth, and emotional well-being back to the experiences they endured as children. The damage is not just personal—it ripples outward, affecting families, relationships, and future generations. I have lived through these struggles, carrying the weight of my past into adulthood, navigating relationships with caution, and questioning whether I was worthy of love and safety.

Speaking out about sexual abuse is an act of profound courage, but it is not without risk. Survivors often face skepticism, scrutiny, or even hostility—especially in communities where reputation, honor, or religious beliefs play a central role. In my experience, the silence in my family and the discomfort in addressing my abuse reinforced my isolation. There were no open discussions, no reassurances that I was not to blame. Instead, I learned early that survival meant enduring in silence.

The stigma surrounding sexual abuse is deeply rooted in cultural norms and harmful misconceptions. Myths about consent, power, and victim behavior continue to shield abusers and discourage survivors from seeking justice. Society too often demands that survivors fit a certain narrative—one of immediate, perfect victimhood—before their pain is acknowledged. Challenging these deeply entrenched norms requires not only education but a willingness to listen and believe survivors, something I wish I had received when I was younger.

Healing from the shame and stigma of sexual abuse requires more than just time—it requires intentional action. Survivors need access to support systems that offer counseling, legal advocacy, and safe spaces for their voices to be heard. Public education must dismantle victim-blaming narratives and shift the focus to holding abusers accountable. For survivors like me, healing also means reclaiming the power that was once taken from us. It means refusing to carry shame that was never ours to bear.

For survivors, reclaiming their voice is an essential step toward healing. Sharing our stories—whether in therapy, through writing, or with trusted loved ones—allows us to break free from the silence that once held us captive. Sexual abuse does not only affect the survivor—it impacts families, friends, and entire communities. Those who support survivors must learn how to respond with compassion, without adding to the shame and doubt so many of us already feel. Education is critical, not just for those who have been harmed but for those who want to create a world where abuse is no longer tolerated in silence. I often wonder how different my journey would have been if those around me had been equipped with the knowledge and courage to truly see and support me.

Faith communities can play a complicated role in a survivor's healing journey. While some offer comfort and understanding, others silence victims, prioritizing forgiveness over justice. I struggled with this tension myself, questioning how to reconcile my pain with the expectation of grace. I have come to believe that true faith does not demand silence from the wounded. Instead, it calls for justice, accountability, and a commitment to ensuring that others do not suffer in the same way.

Equally important is educating adults—parents, teachers, community leaders—on how to recognize the warning signs of abuse. Creating safe environments means making conversations about abuse and protection a normal part of how we raise and care for children.

The legal system remains a daunting barrier for many survivors seeking justice. The process is invasive, often retraumatizing, and outcomes are uncertain. Many victims, knowing the difficulty of proving their abuse, never report it at all. If justice systems are to serve survivors, they must be reformed to prioritize their dignity and well-being rather than reinforcing their trauma.

Despite the challenges, movements like #MeToo have demonstrated the power of collective voices. They have shown that when survivors speak out, we are not just telling our own stories—we are demanding accountability, breaking generational cycles of harm, and creating a safer world for others. Speaking out has shown me that my pain is not just my own. It is a part of a larger narrative, one that so many others share, and one that we have the power to change.

Survivors deserve to live in a world where their voices are valued, where their experiences are acknowledged, and where silence is no longer expected of us. Breaking that silence is not just an act of personal courage—it is a call for justice, for understanding, and for a society that refuses to allow abuse to thrive in the shadows. My journey to healing has been long, but I am no longer bound by the weight of shame. I am free to tell my story, to own my truth, and to remind others that they, too, are not alone.

Forward

with

Fortitude

"Healing may not be so much about getting better,
as about letting go of everything that isn't you—
all of the expectations, all of the beliefs—
and becoming who you are."

—Rachel Naomi Remen

CHAPTER XX

Beyond the Pain, Beyond the Past

> *He heals the brokenhearted*
> *and binds up their wounds.*
>
> ~ Psalm 147:3 (NIV)

I have carried my past with me for so long, often feeling as though I was shackled to it, unable to move forward without dragging the weight of old wounds behind me. The memories—the hurt, the betrayal, the disappointment—were not just recollections but emotional burdens I didn't know how to release. For years, I allowed them to determine how I viewed myself and the world around me. The pain I endured may always be a part of my story, but it no longer controls the narrative of my life.

I am poised to move beyond the pain and the past, no longer bound by the bitterness that once kept me locked in place. While the memories remain, they no longer dictate my future. I choose to focus on the love I have cultivated, the relationships I have strengthened, and the peace I have embraced. For too long, I lived as if I had something to prove—as if my survival depended on constant motion, on staying ahead of my wounds before they could catch up with me. Now, I recognize that true strength is not in avoidance but in acceptance.

There was a time when I mourned the past as if it was the only thing that defined me. I fixated on the pain, replaying the injustices, the disappointments, and the moments I wished had been different. But now, I choose to celebrate what has come from my journey. I have built a life filled with love, family, and purpose. I have found joy in the smallest moments, in laughter shared over dinner, in the warmth of spending time with my grandchildren, my daughter and nieces, in the companionship of my husband. These are the things I will carry forward.

Releasing the hold of the past has also meant embracing self-love in a way I never had before. For years, I viewed myself through the lens of what I had endured rather than through the light of who I had become. It has taken time to unlearn the belief that my worth was tied to my hardships. Today, I affirm my value not because of what I have survived but because of who I am—strong, compassionate, and deeply loved.

I have also learned the importance of setting boundaries—not to shut people out, but to protect my peace. I no longer feel the need to overextend myself, to prove my worth through busyness, or to sacrifice my well-being for the comfort of others. Instead, I prioritize what truly matters, choosing relationships and commitments that align with the life I want to live.

Moving beyond my past does not mean minimizing the effects but rather reframing it as a source of wisdom. Every hardship, every challenge, every tear shed has contributed to the person I am today. And while I no longer dwell on the pain, I honor the lessons it has taught me—the importance of resilience, the power of love, and the gift of faith.

Each day, I remind myself that healing is an ongoing process. There will be moments when the past whispers to me, trying to pull me back into old patterns of doubt or fear. But now, I am equipped with the tools to face those moments with grace. I have the strength to stand firm in who I am, to choose peace over pain, and to embrace the future with confidence.

I have walked through the fire, but I have not been consumed by it. I have emerged with a deeper understanding of myself, my faith, and my purpose. The road ahead is no longer shadowed by what has been but illuminated by what is possible.

"Don't be pushed around by the fears in your mind.

Be led by the dreams in your heart."

— Roy T. Bennett

CHAPTER XXI

My Faith Is Bigger Than My Fear

When I am afraid,
I put my trust in you.

~ Psalm 56:3 (NIV)

F aith has been the cornerstone of my journey, giving me the strength to confront my fears. When I decided to care for Edward, I knew I would face judgment. When I chose to speak openly about my sexual abuse, I anticipated resistance. Yet, in both instances, my faith proved to be bigger than my fear. It was my unwavering belief in God's plan that enabled me to move forward, even when doubt and criticism loomed large.

Faith gives us the courage to confront what we fear most. For me, that meant facing the possibility of rejection and misunderstanding. It meant stepping into the light with my story, even when it felt safer to stay in the shadows. My faith reminded me that I wasn't walking this path alone. God was with me, guiding me every step of the way.

As others questioned why I would extend myself for someone who had caused me so much pain, their skepticism mirrored my own internal struggles. But my faith reminded me that forgiveness and love are more powerful than bitterness and resentment. I trusted that God had a purpose for this part of my life, even if others couldn't understand it. Choosing to care for someone who had hurt me was an act of faith that challenged me to embody the principles of love and forgiveness. It wasn't easy, but it was necessary for my healing and for his.

The fear of judgment is a natural barrier to revealing one's true self and can be paralyzing, but faith can help us overcome it. And, gaining freedom from the need for approval allows us to live in alignment with our values. Speaking about my sexual abuse was one of the scariest acts of my life. I worried about how people would perceive me. Would they see me as broken? Would they pity me? I have embraced the opinion that our worth is not determined by the viewpoints of others, but by our alignment with God's purpose.

My faith has been my anchor, keeping me grounded in the truth of who I am and what I'm called to do. Faith is a powerful antidote to fear, and it gives us the strength to confront our pain, the courage to share our stories, and the resilience to face scrutiny.

The most difficult experiences can serve a greater purpose, guiding us through challenges and reminding us that God's plan is far greater than the thoughts of others. The decision to speak openly about my abuse was not an easy one, but it was necessary.

I trusted that my experiences could help others, and that God would use my story to bring hope to those in need. This belief sustains me as I continue to share my experiences and to help others find their own paths to healing. I hope to create spaces where others feel empowered to begin their own healing journeys.

I've learned to see my pain as a tool for growth. Each challenge I've faced has been an opportunity to lean on God's strength and to grow in resilience. This perspective has allowed me to find meaning in my experiences and to use them to help others.

My faith is a guiding light that leads me through the darkness and toward a place of reflection and healing. It has been my anchor, helping me to navigate the complexities of my journey and to find peace along the way.

God's plan is always the best.

Sometimes the process is painful and hard.

But don't forget that when God is silent,

He is doing something good for you.

— Josh Woolums

CHAPTER XXII

Understanding God's Plan in Pain

And we know that in all things God works for the good of those who love him, who have been called according to his purpose.

~ Romans 8:28 (NIV)

I traveled to Greenville, N.C., multiple times a week during Edward's hospital stay. Each visit was emotionally draining but necessary. I felt an obligation to be present for him during this critical time. Sometimes, I spent the night at a hotel to recover from the toll of the journey and the emotional weight of the visits. Other times, when Alvin was able to accompany me, we made the eight-hour round-trip drive in a single day. The logistics were exhausting, but I couldn't imagine not showing up. When I was unable to be physically present, I remained in constant communication with his nursing team. Every update mattered. Knowing the details of his care helped me feel somewhat in control of an otherwise overwhelming situation.

If I wasn't at the hospital, Edward and I had grown close enough that he felt comfortable calling me multiple times a day. These calls were a mix of updates, questions, and moments of shared vulnerability. They were evidence of the trust we had built. I worked closely with his care team to identify a skilled nursing facility for him to transition to after discharge. It was clear his previous residence was unsuitable, and I wanted to ensure he would be in a place where he'd feel safe and supported.

Discussions about treatment options were difficult. The medical team determined that chemotherapy wasn't viable due to the size and location of Edward's tumors. The prognosis was bleak: three months without treatment. It was a painful reality to accept. Life outside the hospital didn't stop. Three weeks after my first visit to the hospital I had to travel to Houston, Texas, for a day to manage some personal business. While I was there, I received a call from the nursing staff informing me that Edward had suffered a seizure.

The call required an immediate decision. They asked if I wanted him intubated. I declined, instructing them to stabilize him and prioritize his comfort. It was a moment of clarity amidst the chaos, though it weighed heavily on me. When I returned to the hospital the next day, Edward was in a semi-comatose state. His ability to communicate was reduced to faint, garbled words. It was heart-wrenching to see him in that condition.

The medical team advised that hospice was the only viable option at this stage. Although I had some support from family, I felt it was a decision I needed to make on my own. I wanted to ensure there were no alternatives before agreeing to this course. Once Edward was moved to hospice, I stayed by his side for the first few days. I played gospel music softly in the background, held his hand, and gently rubbed his head. I hoped these small gestures brought him comfort.

Though Edward's awareness was limited, there were fleeting moments when he seemed to recognize my presence. He called my name in a distorted tone, and those moments felt like fragile yet precious gifts. The hospice team administered medication to keep him comfortable. While his physical pain was managed, my emotional pain grew. I found myself in need of a break to process everything that was happening.

My husband was out of town on a planned trip, so I returned home alone on a Friday afternoon to a quiet, empty house. The silence was both a reprieve and a reminder of the enormity of what lay ahead. I planned to return to the hospice site on Sunday morning. However, on Saturday night, September 30, 2023, I received a call from the Chaplain. Edward had passed away peacefully. I sat in silence, the weight of the news settling over me. It felt surreal, as though time had stopped.

After a moment, I began notifying family members. I called Alvin, Mary, Arthur Jr., and Chantell to inform them of Edward's passing. Speaking those words out loud solidified the reality of his death. Without much time to grieve, I shifted into planning mode. Practical tasks needed to be handled, and I threw myself into them to keep from dwelling on my emotions.

I contacted the funeral home in Jacksonville, N.C., and instructed them to retrieve his remains. On Monday morning, I drove to Jacksonville to make the funeral arrangements. I wrote the obituary, went through his telephone to retrieve pictures, ordered him a suit, and selected the casket and burial plot. Each decision felt heavy, yet I moved through the motions, ensuring that his final arrangements were handled with care.

The funeral brought unexpected moments of reflection. Several of Edward's friends spoke on his behalf, sharing stories that painted a different picture of the man I had known. One gentleman recounted how Edward had started attending church with him in recent months. I wondered if he had sought God's forgiveness during those visits. People from his job sent flowers, and others spoke of his kindness and sense of humor. A close friend of his even prepared multiple dishes for the repast.

It was hard to reconcile my experience of Edward with the memories shared by his friends and associates. Yet, it was clear he was loved by many. This realization gave me a measure of comfort, though the contrast with my own experience was striking. Mary wasn't well enough to attend the funeral, so from the family, it was myself, Alvin, my brother Arthur Jr., and my nephew Jerrell who were present. My daughter and nieces wanted to attend, but I knew their gesture was more for me than for him, and I didn't want them to become emotionally distraught. I asked them to stay home.

To my surprise, my cousins from Georgia walked into the funeral home. They didn't know the history of Edward's actions, and I was grateful for their presence. Their support reminded me of the strength found in family, even when the dynamics are complicated.

Seeing Edward in the casket was surreal. He looked at peace, but the image was a stark reminder of the journey that had led us here. I delivered a speech during the service, reflecting on forgiveness, grace, and the bond we had rebuilt. It was both a tribute to him and a testament to the healing process we had undergone together.

Despite the sadness, I felt a quiet sense of fulfillment. I had honored Edward in his final days and in his passing. It was a moment of grace amidst the grief. The experience forced me to confront my own vulnerabilities and strengths. It was a reminder that healing does not follow a direct course, but one marked by grace and resilience.

CHAPTER XXIII

Unintentional Grief: The Hidden Impact

> *Grief, I've learned,*
> *is really just love.*
> *It's all the love you want*
> *to give but cannot.*
>
> ~ Jamie Anderson

I often felt like I was running on autopilot while attending to Edward's needs. Caring for him blurred the lines between past and present. Memories of my childhood—ones I thought I had locked away for good—resurfaced. These memories didn't just haunt me; they intertwined with my grief, making it harder to separate my current emotions from the pain of my past. This intermingling created a unique emotional weight, one that felt like both a dismissal of my pain and an acknowledgment of my humanity.

The demands of the task kept my mind occupied, leaving little room to process the emotions swirling beneath the surface. Most of the time,

I was so focused on making decisions, managing his care, and ensuring he was comfortable that I didn't have the bandwidth to acknowledge my own feelings. It wasn't until after his death that the weight of everything began to hit me hard.

The quiet moments, once filled with the urgency of caregiving, now felt overwhelming as the reality of his absence set in. I began to understand the concept of unintentional grief—grief that emerges unexpectedly, sneaking up on you when you least expect it and leaving a profound emotional impact. It was as though all the emotions I had pushed aside while staying strong for Edward were now demanding to be felt.

For me, unintentional grief began as a quiet undercurrent. It surfaced in the sadness I felt watching Edward's physical decline, the compassion I couldn't help but feel despite our complicated past, and the guilt that accompanied any semblance of mourning for him. It wasn't a conscious choice to grieve; the emotions appeared unbidden, unwelcomed, yet undeniably real.

Unintentional grief also tested the boundaries of forgiveness. While I had made the decision to forgive Edward, caring for him brought unresolved anger and resentment to the surface. This grief forced me to confront my lingering wounds, making the path to healing feel even more complicated. Yet, it also reshaped my perspective. I learned that emotions are not always logical. Sometimes, they exist simultaneously, creating a messy but valid tapestry of feelings.

Grief, even when it sneaks up on us, is deeply human. I often found myself crying alone, unable to share these feelings with others. The isolation compounded my emotional burden. I worried that expressing my sadness might confuse those around me or make them question my resolve. So, I tucked the emotions away, letting them surface only in private moments.

My self-imposed isolation deepened the challenge of navigating unintentional grief. I feared judgment and misunderstanding if I shared my emotions openly. This silence created loneliness, making the grief feel even heavier. I longed for connection but couldn't find the words to explain what I was experiencing. The inner critic amplified this struggle, questioning my strength and resilience and feeding into the shame I already felt.

For survivors of trauma, mourning someone who caused harm can feel especially fraught. Before Edward died, I had struggled to reconcile my sadness for his condition with the adverse feelings I still carried. These conflicting emotions created a whirlwind inside me, one I couldn't fully articulate. Grieving for Edward felt also felt like mourning the sibling relationship we should have had, a bond untainted by betrayal. This grief wasn't just unintentional—it felt inevitable, a byproduct of unmet hopes and fractured ties.

The physical manifestations of grief added another layer of complexity. I felt fatigued, tense, and burdened by headaches—as if my body mourned alongside my mind. These symptoms reminded me that grief, whether intentional or not, demands to be felt, even when we try to suppress it.

Unintentional grief also brought unexpected lessons in compassion. While I couldn't condone Edward's actions, I found myself empathizing with his suffering. This empathy reminded me of the humanity that exists even in those who have caused harm. It was a delicate balance, one that required strength and self-awareness.

I also needed to face difficult questions: What does it mean to grieve for someone who hurt you? How do you honor your own pain while acknowledging their humanity? These reflections became a vital part of my healing process. They taught me that grieving—even unintentionally—is not a sign of weakness. Instead, it's a testament to the complexity of human emotions.

Grief has a way of altering our perspectives, offering lessons that we might not have sought but desperately needed. It peels back the layers of our defenses, exposing the raw and vulnerable parts of ourselves. Through this process, I discovered truths about my capacity for strength, my ability to forgive, and my resilience in the face of adversity. Grief became a mirror reflecting the depth of my humanity and my capacity to love despite the scars.

Over time, I began to acknowledge this grief without judgment. I stopped trying to categorize it as "right" or "wrong" and accepted it as a natural response to a complicated situation. This acceptance was freeing, allowing me to process my emotions more fully. Journaling provided a safe space to explore the tangled web of sadness, guilt, and compassion defining this chapter of my life.

Learning to coexist with grief meant embracing it as a part of my story rather than something to be hidden away. It required patience and grace, allowing myself to feel its weight without being consumed by it. The journey was not direct; there were moments when the sadness felt overwhelming, but with time, I learned to accept those feelings as evidence of growth and healing.

In many ways, grief became a bridge—connecting the person I was with the person I am becoming. It taught me to see beyond the surface of my pain, uncovering the beauty and strength that lay beneath. Through grief, I developed a deeper appreciation for the moments of joy and connection. It has shown me that even amidst sorrow, there is room for hope and gratitude.

This unintentional teacher has also reminded me of the importance of self-compassion. Too often, we are harsh critics of our own healing process, expecting to move on quickly or without lingering emotions.

Grief taught me to be gentle with myself, to recognize that healing is not a destination but a journey. By embracing this truth, I found the courage to face each day with an open heart and an unwavering belief in my ability to overcome.

Ultimately, the lessons of grief have shaped me into a more compassionate and empathetic person. They have deepened my understanding of what it means to be human—to feel deeply, to endure, and to rise. This path has reaffirmed that we are not defined by the wounds we carry but by the love and strength we cultivate in their aftermath. Grief, though challenging, has become a transformative force, guiding me toward a place of renewed purpose and inner peace.

In the end, unintentional grief became a teacher. It showed me that healing is not about erasing pain but about learning to coexist with it. This grief, though challenging, became a bridge to deeper self-awareness and resilience. It reminded me that we are not defined by what we endure but by how we choose to move forward.

"Your faith will be tested
right before your breakthrough.
Keep your head held high and remain positive;
regardless of what hurdles may come your way.
You have the ability to successfully jump over them."

— Robin S. Baker

CHAPTER XXIV

A Test of Faith

> *Weeping may endure for a night,*
> *but joy comes in the morning.*
>
> ~ Psalm 30:5 (NKJV)

In December of 2024, just months after Edward passed away, my family and I were preparing for a long-anticipated trip to Amsterdam and Belgium. It was meant to be a reprieve, a chance to breathe after the emotional toll of Edward's death. But life had other plans. My sister Mary was hospitalized due to a COPD exacerbation just days before we were set to leave. Her health was already fragile, and this sudden setback cast a shadow over our plans.

The medical team's focus was on stabilizing her oxygen levels and keeping her CO_2 levels down. For the first few days, she responded well to the treatment. We were able to talk on the phone, and she assured me she was doing okay. The doctors were optimistic, saying she would be discharged once she stabilized. I clung to that hope, praying that this would be just another hurdle she would overcome, as she had so many times before.

But just as quickly as hope had appeared, it was dashed. Four days after we left for our trip, Mary's condition took a sudden turn. I received the devastating news that she had been intubated and transferred to the Intensive Care Unit. My heart sank. Her carbon dioxide levels skyrocketed to dangerous levels, and the medical team's concerns deepened. I felt a deep sense of guilt for not being there, for being so far away when she needed me most.

Jerrell, Mary's son, and Kaminisha, my niece, stepped in to keep me updated. They became my lifeline to Mary's situation. Every phone call was a mixture of hope and dread. Each update seemed worse than the last. The situation spiraled quickly, and before I could process what was happening, the unthinkable occurred. Mary passed away on December 30, exactly 90 days after Edward. As the year ended, so did Mary's life.

We were in Belgium when we got the news. Devastation doesn't even begin to describe what I felt. I was already reeling from Edward's loss, still processing the pain and trauma of his passing. Losing Mary felt like another piece of my soul being torn away. She was my last surviving sister. Gwen had passed away in 2006, Joyce in 2016, and now Mary was gone. The weight of being the only sister left was unbearable.

I felt like I was in a nightmare I couldn't wake up from. My heart was shattered, and my faith felt nonexistent. How could I endure this? How could I keep going when loss after loss seemed to be the only constant in my life? I questioned everything I believed in. My trust in God, my faith in His plan—it all felt like it was slipping through my fingers.

When we returned to the States, I went into autopilot. It was the only way I could function. There was so much to do, and I couldn't let myself feel—not yet. As though I was in repeat mode from arranging services for Edward, I planned Mary's funeral, wrote her obituary, picked out her casket, met with the cemetery and the funeral home. Every decision felt like a dagger to my heart. Each task brought me closer to the reality that Mary was truly gone.

I moved through the motions, but inside, I was numb. I had spent so much time processing the situation with Edward, and now I was thrust into mourning Mary. It felt like there was no room to breathe, no space to process one loss before another came crashing down. The weight of it all was suffocating.

My faith, which had always been my anchor, felt shattered. I couldn't find solace in prayer or scripture. The words felt hollow, the promises of peace and comfort distant. I'd always believed in God's plan, but now, I questioned it. Why would He take so much from me? Why would He leave me to navigate this unbearable pain?

The loss of Mary forced me to confront my grief in a way I hadn't with Edward. With Edward, I had been consumed by the logistics of his care and his passing. But with Mary, I was left with the raw, unfiltered reality of being the last sister standing. The memories of our childhood, our shared experiences, and our bond—they were all mine now, with no one to share them with. The emptiness was overwhelming.

As I stood in the funeral home, planning for Mary, I felt like I was floating outside of my body. It was as if I was watching someone else go through the motions. I couldn't connect to the emotions, couldn't let myself feel the full weight of the loss. To do so would have been too much to bear.

The funeral was a blur. I remember the faces of family and friends, their kind words and condolences. But it all felt distant, like a scene from a movie. I smiled when I was supposed to, nodded at the right moments, but inside, I felt hollow. The grief was too deep, too raw to express.

In the weeks that followed, I struggled to find my footing. The world kept moving, but I felt stuck in place, trapped in a whirlwind of pain and doubt. My faith, which had always been my guiding light, was dim.

I couldn't bring myself to pray. The words felt empty, the act pointless. How could I talk to God when I felt so betrayed by Him?

I knew I couldn't stay in that place forever. Slowly, I began to lean on the support of my family and friends. They became my lifeline, reminding me that I wasn't alone, even when it felt like I was. Their presence was a balm for my soul, a reminder that there was still love and light in the world, even in times of darkness.

I also began to seek solace in the memories of my sisters. Gwen, Joyce, and Mary had been such integral parts of my life, and their absence was a void that could never be filled. But I found comfort in remembering the good times, the laughter, and the love we shared. Those memories became a source of strength, a reminder that their spirits lived on in me.

The journey is not easy, there are days when the pain feels insurmountable, and the grief threatens to consume me. But little by little, I am rebuilding my faith. I started to pray again, not with the expectation of answers, but with the hope of finding peace. I turned to scripture, searching for passages that spoke to my heart, that reminded me of God's love and His promise to never leave me.

One verse that resonated deeply with me was Psalm 34:18: "The Lord is close to the brokenhearted and saves those who are crushed in spirit." I clung to those words, repeating them to myself on the darkest days. They became a lifeline, a reminder that even in my pain, God was there, holding me up when I couldn't stand on my own.

The journey through grief takes unexpected turns and unfolds in ways we can hardly predict. There are good days and bad days, moments of clarity and moments of despair. But through it all, I've learned the importance of leaning on my faith, even when it feels fragile. I've learned that it's okay to question, to doubt, and to wrestle with God. Those moments of struggle have brought me closer to Him, helping me to see that even in my brokenness, I am loved.

Losing Mary was a test of faith unlike any I've ever faced. It forced me to confront my pain, my doubts, and my fears head-on. But it also taught me the power of resilience, the strength of community, and the enduring presence of God's love. Her passing was a loss I will carry with me for the rest of my life, but it was also a turning point—a moment that reminded me of the importance of faith, even in the face of unimaginable pain.

"You will not experience dramatic change in your struggle as long as you use accountability to describe your sins instead of declaring your need for help in the midst of temptation."

— Heath Lambert

CHAPTER XXV

The Connection Between Faith and Therapy

Prayer is powerful, but so is therapy. Healing happens when we allow both God's grace and the tools He provides to work in our lives.

~ Dr. Anita Phillips

As a young adult, I brought up therapy in a conversation with my mother, and she looked at me as if I'd spoken a foreign language. "Therapy?" she repeated, her brow furrowing. "What do you need that for? You just need to pray harder." Her words were not malicious; they were rooted in a deep-seated belief system that faith alone could cure all wounds.

For generations, the Black community has relied on faith as a source of strength, a refuge in times of hardship. But while prayer is powerful, it does not negate the need for professional mental health support. Instead, it can work alongside therapy to foster deeper healing. My mother's response was not uncommon—it echoed a broader cultural belief that therapy is unnecessary, that seeking outside help is a sign of weakness, or worse, a lack of faith.

The stigma surrounding therapy often suppresses the voices of those who need it most. Many Black families, including my own, were taught to endure struggles quietly, convinced that seeking help would make them appear weak or unfaithful. This reluctance is rooted in historical and cultural experiences, where resilience has been essential for survival.

Black Americans have faced systemic oppression, racial trauma, and economic instability for generations—circumstances that have often left them with no choice but to rely on faith and community as their primary means of coping (Williams et al., 2020). Yet, while these support systems provide invaluable comfort, they do not replace professional intervention. I've witnessed the life-changing power of therapy—not as a substitute for faith, but as a complement to it, offering practical tools to navigate life's complexities. Therapy requires faith—faith in the process, in the therapist, and most importantly, in oneself.

For many in the Black community, the church is more than a place of worship; it is a cultural and social hub. Historically, it has provided not only spiritual guidance but also emotional and financial support. Pastors often serve as counselors, offering advice on everything from relationships to grief and mental health. But while pastors are deeply trusted figures, most are not trained mental health professionals. There is a limit to how much they can help, and without professional intervention, serious mental health issues can go unaddressed. Unfortunately, because the church has long been the foundation of emotional support, many believe that seeking therapy means turning away from faith. This misconception keeps people from getting the help they need. Recognizing the limitations of spiritual guidance does not diminish its importance; rather, it highlights the need for a holistic approach—one that embraces faith while also utilizing professional mental health resources.

Access to therapy in the Black community is further complicated by systemic barriers. Many Black individuals face difficulties in finding a therapist who understands their cultural background and experiences. Research shows that Black Americans are less likely than White Americans to receive mental health treatment, and when they do, they often encounter providers who lack cultural competence (Bailey et al., 2017).

The lack of Black mental health professionals creates an additional hurdle—many Black individuals feel that a non-Black therapist may not fully grasp the nuances of their lived experience, including racial trauma and generational burdens. When I first considered therapy, I struggled with the idea of opening up to someone who might not understand my background, my family dynamics, or the cultural expectations that shaped my silence. The need for culturally responsive therapy is critical in addressing the unique challenges Black individuals face. Without it, many people feel misunderstood or dismissed, reinforcing the idea that therapy is not meant for them.

Another major obstacle is the widespread belief that therapy is not for Black people. This idea is deeply ingrained, stemming from both historical distrust of the medical system and the belief that mental health struggles should be handled privately or within the family. Black people have historically been subjected to medical racism, misdiagnosis, and mistreatment in healthcare settings, further discouraging them from seeking professional help (Henderson et al., 2021).

As a result, many within the community are hesitant to trust therapists, fearing judgment or invalidation. This fear keeps people suffering in silence, afraid to confront their pain in a therapeutic setting. But choosing therapy is not a betrayal of our culture or our faith—it is an investment in our well-being. The same way we would seek a doctor for physical ailments, we must be willing to seek professional help for emotional and psychological wounds.

After the devastating loss of two siblings within a 90-day period, I realized I needed more than prayer alone to navigate the overwhelming weight of my grief. Losing one sibling is painful enough, but losing two in such a short time brought a grief so layered and complex that it felt impossible to untangle. The loss unearthed unresolved emotions, magnified old wounds, and left me grappling with questions I wasn't prepared to answer. I turned to prayer, searching for comfort in my faith, but I also recognized that I needed guidance beyond what prayer alone could offer. I had to face my grief head-on, to process it with intention. Therapy became that space for me. It gave me a structure to work through my pain while still allowing my faith to be my anchor.

When I attended therapy after my siblings' deaths, I sought to supplement my faith, not replace it. While prayer offered me solace, therapy gave me the tools to understand the depths of my grief and unpack the pain I was carrying. It helped me face the intricacies of loss—the anger, the guilt, the confusion—and address them in a way that strengthened my faith rather than weakened it.

Therapy was not an admission of doubt; it was a commitment to healing. I wasn't just praying about my struggles; I was actively working through them, understanding them, and learning to live with them. That distinction made all the difference. Faith and therapy are not opposing forces; they are allies in healing. Together, they address the mind, body, and spirit, creating a comprehensive approach to well-being.

One of the most promising developments in mental health care is the integration of faith-based counseling with traditional therapy. Many mental health professionals now offer services that incorporate spirituality into treatment, recognizing that for many, faith is a central pillar of their identity. Faith-based therapy allows individuals to process their emotions while still grounding themselves in their beliefs. For those who struggle with the idea of therapy, faith-based approaches can make the process feel more accessible.

By bridging the gap between spiritual and psychological care, more people in the Black community may feel empowered to seek help. This approach does not diminish the role of faith—it *enhances* it, offering people the tools they need to heal while remaining deeply connected to their spiritual values.

True strength lies in vulnerability, in acknowledging our pain and seeking help to heal it. Faith can be strengthened through therapy when approached with openness and a willingness to grow. Therapy requires courage—a readiness to confront the parts of ourselves we often keep hidden. It creates space for transparent discussions, allowing us to examine our emotions, beliefs, and experiences with honesty. By integrating faith and therapy, we can create a future where healing is not a choice between the two, but a combination that allows us to thrive.

To anyone struggling with challenges in life, I offer this: therapy isn't a rejection of faith; it's an extension of it. It's an act of faith in yourself and in the belief that healing is possible. When I pray now, I feel more connected, more open. Therapy has taught me to articulate my feelings, understand my triggers, and approach my prayers with clarity and intention. Faith gave me the foundation, and therapy helped me build upon it. Together, they have shaped my healing journey in ways I never imagined possible.

Let's change the narrative around what "strong black woman" means. … Strong black women are admirable in our strengths and contributions! We can fulfill our purpose by re-filling ourselves through self-care!

— Cortney Downs, MSW, CSW

CHAPTER XXVI

Understanding the Myth of the Strong Black Woman

> *You don't have to be perfect to be strong. You just have to be willing to keep going.*
>
> ~ Michelle Obama

I have spent my entire life being the strong woman—the girlfriend, the sister, the wife, the mother, the auntie, the employee—who has the capacity to handle any circumstance at any time. This ability to carry everything and everyone is both a gift and a burden, one that I have come to recognize as deeply rooted in resilience, strength, and trauma (Harris-Perry, 2011). Black women have been conditioned, because of lived experiences, to "hold everything down," cry through pain, and hide our tears.

Our strength has always been necessary—for our families, our communities, and our survival. And so, when Edward became ill, stepping in to care for him felt inevitable. It didn't matter what he had done to me, what scars I carried, or how heavy the emotional toll would be. I pushed through, because that is what I had always done. But now, looking back, I understand that my actions were not just about faith, duty, or forgiveness—they were also a reflection of the myth of the Strong Black Woman (SBW) that I had unknowingly internalized my entire life.

The SBW myth is one that glorifies our ability to endure pain, to carry more than our fair share, and to sacrifice ourselves for the well-being of others. This narrative was ingrained in me from childhood, watching the women in my life navigate hardship with grace and unwavering perseverance. I saw my mother make impossible decisions to protect us. I watched my sisters balance work, family, and personal struggles without ever showing cracks in their armor.

And so, without realizing it, I became that woman, too—the one who handles everything. When my brother lay dying, I took on his care, his comfort, and even his dignity, because I believed it was the right thing to do. And it was. But it was also a continuation of a lifetime of putting everyone else's needs before my own, often at the expense of my own well-being.

Black women are socialized to believe that vulnerability is a luxury we cannot afford. We internalize the idea that we must be strong at all costs, that breaking down is not an option, and that prioritizing ourselves is selfish. This belief is deeply embedded in both history and survival, stemming from generations of oppression where Black women were required to be caretakers and laborers, often without acknowledgment or rest (Beauboeuf-Lafontant, 2009).

When I chose to care for Edward, there was no question in my mind that I could do it. I had done hard things before, and this was just another test of my endurance. But what I never stopped to ask myself was: should

I have to? Was this my burden to carry alone? And what was the cost of always being the person who says yes?

Faith has always been my guiding source, the foundation that allows me to "just do it," even when the weight is unbearable. I have always believed that God gives me the strength to endure, to push forward, to serve. And I do not regret that faith or that calling—it has shaped who I am. But I also recognize that faith should not be a justification for self-ne-glect. Somewhere along the way, I stopped distinguishing between faith and over-functioning.

I assumed that just because I could bear it, it meant I was supposed to. I now understand that God did not create me to be a martyr for everyone else's well-being while ignoring my own. Strength should not be synonymous with suffering, and yet, for so many Black women, it is (Abrams et al., 2014).

The reality is that strong Black women often have no space for weak-ness. There is an unspoken expectation that we will not break, that we will always figure it out, that we will keep pushing forward no matter how much it costs us. This expectation is not just placed on us by oth-ers—it is something we place on ourselves. And the consequences are serious. Research has shown that the stress of constantly demonstrat-ing strength leads to higher rates of hypertension, cardiovascular dis-ease, anxiety, depression, and other health complications among Black women (Woods-Giscombe, 2010).

The resilience that keeps us going is the same resilience that can break us down. I see this now. And I am learning that it is okay to take the cape off. Trauma has a way of convincing us that we must overcompensate—for our past, for our wounds, for our fear of being seen as weak. I have spent decades proving my worth through my actions, by taking care of others, by never saying no.

Where did that come from? Was I trying to prove that I was stronger than my trauma? Was I trying to erase my pain by ensuring that no one could ever say I wasn't good enough? The more I reflect, the more I see that my need to handle everything was never just about being strong—it was about avoiding my own pain. If I stayed busy fixing everyone else's problems, I never had to sit with my own.

But I am sitting with them now. I am looking at the cost of my strength. And I am choosing a different path. I am taking off my cape. I am learning how to rest. I am holding others—family, friends, associates, and others—accountable for their own well-being. I no longer believe that I must be the only one who shows up. Others are just as capable and must learn to carry their own weight. And I must learn to prioritize myself without guilt.

For the first time, I am giving myself permission to ask: what do I need? Not what my family needs. Not what others expect. What do I need to be whole, to be healthy, to be free? The answer to that question will shape the rest of my life. Because strength is not just about endurance—it is also about knowing when to stop carrying things that no longer serve you.

And I am ready to let go.

CHAPTER XXVII

The Courage to Heal Out Loud

Owning our story and loving ourselves through that process is the bravest thing that we will ever do.

~ Brené Brown

I knew that I wanted to inspire and uplift people by openly sharing my story—I wanted to *heal out loud*. It wasn't an easy choice, and it wasn't one I made lightly. For years, I had carried the weight of guilt, secrecy, and the pressure to appear strong. To the world, I was a hard-charging, accomplished, polished, high-achieving individual. But beneath that veneer of success was a woman struggling with the scars of her past.

When I first entertained the idea of sharing my story, I was gripped by fear. What would people think? Would they judge me? Would my vulnerability undermine the respect I had worked so hard to earn? These questions kept me up at night. But as I wrestled with my doubts, I realized that staying silent was no longer an option. My story, as painful as it was, had the power to inspire others to confront their own pain and find healing.

The turning point came when I was invited to deliver a TEDx talk. The opportunity felt like both a gift and a challenge. I decided to title my talk "Healing Out Loud." The name itself felt like a declaration, a promise to myself and to others that I would no longer hide. Preparing for the talk was an emotional process. I had to revisit parts of my story that I had tucked away, parts I wasn't sure I was ready to share.

As I worked on my speech, I felt a mix of emotions: fear, anxiety, and, surprisingly, relief. Writing the talk forced me to confront my own shame and the ways it had held me back. I realized that by hiding my story, I had been feeding the very shame I wanted to escape. The act of putting my experiences into words was cathartic. It was as if each sentence I wrote loosened the grip of shame just a little more.

The day of the talk arrived, and I was nervous in a way I hadn't been in years. I've spoken in front of audiences before, but this was different. This time, I wasn't just sharing knowledge or expertise—I was sharing my heart. The speaker who went before me froze at three different intervals in her speech, which only heightened my anxiety. I was the second speaker, and I was petrified. As I stepped onto the stage, the lights were blinding, and for a moment, I wanted to turn back. But then I saw the faces in the audience, and my eyes met Alvin's; he gave me a smile and a nod of encouragement, and I remembered why I was there.

I began to speak, and as the words flowed, something incredible happened. The fear that had gripped me began to melt away. I felt an overwhelming sense of freedom, as if by speaking from my heart, I was reclaiming a part of myself that had been lost. I shared my experiences, my struggles, and my journey to forgiveness and healing. I spoke about the shame I had carried and how it had affected my life. And I spoke about the courage it took to let go of that shame.

When I finished, the room was silent for a moment. Then, one by one, people began to stand and applaud. The applause was deafening, but what moved me even more were the conversations that followed. Audience members approached me with tears in their eyes, sharing their own stories of pain and resilience. Some said my talk had given them the courage to face their own pasts. Others simply thanked me for being transparent.

In the weeks that followed, I received messages from people who had seen my talk online. They told me how my story had inspired them to start their own journeys of healing. Each message felt like a validation of my decision to share. It reinforced the idea that vulnerability is not a weakness but a strength. By sharing my story, I had created a space for others to share theirs, and in doing so, I had found a new sense of purpose.

The experience of "healing out loud" was therapeutic. For so long, I had kept my pain hidden, believing that silence was the price of strength. But in sharing my story, I discovered that strength comes from authenticity. By owning my truth, I was able to release the shame that had weighed me down for so long.

Sharing my story also deepened my empathy for others. I began to see the pain behind the polished exteriors that so many of us present to the world. I realized that everyone is carrying something, and that by sharing our stories, we can lighten each other's loads.

My own healing has deepened. Each time I speak about my experiences, I feel a little freer. It was as if each telling was a step further away from the pain and closer to the person I wanted to be. The act of sharing transformed my wounds into wisdom, my pain into purpose.

I also learned to forgive myself. For years, I had been so hard on myself, criticizing every perceived flaw and failure. Sharing my story forced me to confront those negative thoughts and replace them with compassion. I began to see myself not as someone who had failed, but as someone who had survived and grown.

This journey wasn't just about me. It was about creating a ripple effect, inspiring others to find their own courage to heal out loud. I started receiving invitations to speak at events and workshops, where I met people who were ready to release their own shame and step into their truth. Each interaction reminded me of the power of storytelling and the healing it can bring.

One of the most rewarding moments came when a young woman approached me after a talk at a conference in California. She told me that hearing my story had given her the courage to confront a painful chapter in her own life. "I felt like you were speaking directly to me," she said, tears streaming down her face. Her words reminded me why I had chosen to share my story in the first place.

The courage to heal out loud is not something that comes easily. It requires confronting fears, challenging societal expectations, and stepping into vulnerability. But it is also one of the most liberating experiences I've ever had. It allowed me to reclaim my narrative, to find strength in my story, and to inspire others to do the same.

Healing out loud is a radical act of self-love and community care. It's a way of saying, "I refuse to be defined by my pain." It's a way of breaking the chains of shame and stepping into freedom. And for me, it was a way of turning my pain into a source of hope and inspiration for others.

I have come a long way. The woman who once hid behind a facade of perfection is now someone who embraces her imperfections and uses them to connect with others. The decision to share my story was one of the hardest I've ever made, but it was also one of the most rewarding.

As I continue my work, I am reminded of the words of Brené Brown: "Owning our story and loving ourselves through that process is the bravest thing we'll ever do." These words resonate deeply with me because they capture the essence of what it means to heal out loud.

My story is more than a personal journey—it's a testament to resilience, courage, and the transformative power of honesty. I share it with the hope that others will feel empowered to begin their own healing, to let go of shame, and to stand confidently in their truth. When we choose to heal out loud, we offer others the courage to do the same. Together, we can create a world where healing is embraced, connection is nurtured, and love becomes the foundation for growth.

"You are enough.

You have nothing to prove to anybody."

— Maya Angelou

CHAPTER XXVIII

Speaking Truth to Power: I Am Enough

> *Let us not grow weary in doing good,*
> *for at the proper time we will reap a*
> *harvest if we do not give up.*
>
> ~ Galatians 6:9 (NIV)

Although I have achieved much in my life, I struggled for years with low self-esteem and a persistent sense of being an imposter. The shame from the abuse I endured as a child left me deeply believing that I wasn't good enough or smart enough. This manifested as imposter syndrome—a constant feeling of inadequacy, even as I reached milestone after milestone.

Growing up, I carried a deep sense of responsibility. I was the one who had to get everything right, stay strong, and lead by example. In my mind, failure was never an option. While this mindset drove me to significant success, it also came at a steep cost. I became powered by a relentless cycle of striving for perfection.

Focusing on the next big goal became my coping mechanism—a way to validate my worth and suppress the pain I carried. While I thrived professionally, this unrelenting pursuit left me emotionally and physically drained. For those with similar experiences, the need for control often becomes a survival strategy. For me, it showed up as perfectionism: an unyielding drive to excel in every aspect of my life. As a child, I believed that if I could just be "good enough," I might regain a sense of safety and approval. But perfectionism became both my shield and my prison, guarding me against exposure while distancing me from genuine connections.

On the surface, my ambition brought countless successes—breaking barriers as the first Black chief of staff for the Louisiana Department of Children and Family Services, becoming the first Black female regional general manager in San Diego, serving as assistant director for Riverside's Department of Public Social Services, and earning a doctorate while managing a grueling 60-hour workweek. Yet beneath these accomplishments was a desperate attempt to quiet my insecurities and prove my worth. I often felt unworthy of the recognition I received.

The road to practicing self-kindness has been one of the most significant lessons of my journey. For years, I encouraged others, especially the women I mentored, to forgive themselves, embrace their imperfections, and extend themselves the grace they so freely gave others. Yet I struggled to follow my own advice. I questioned whether I deserved gentleness, as the pain and trauma I endured had convinced me that kindness was something I had to earn.

When I began mentoring women I began to confront my lack of self-kindness. Many of them voiced struggles that mirrored my own—feeling like failures, believing they weren't enough, and being unable to forgive themselves for their mistakes. I would listen and offer reassurance: "You're human. You're allowed to make mistakes. You're worthy of grace." Then, I began to internalize my own words.

Practicing self-kindness wasn't easy—it required unlearning years of self-criticism and embracing my imperfections. Reflective writing became a powerful tool in this process. I began writing letters to myself, acknowledging my efforts, celebrating my progress, and offering myself the understanding I had long denied. Through this practice, I reconnected with my inner self and began to heal.

Sharing my struggles with others also played a pivotal role. When I admitted to the women I mentored that I often struggled with self-kindness, their responses were overwhelmingly supportive. Their vulnerability inspired me to continue being honest about my journey, creating a space for collective healing and growth.

When old patterns still resurface at times, I remind myself of my own words: "You're human. You're allowed to make mistakes. You're worthy of grace." Each time I practice self-affirmation; I reinforce the belief that I am enough.

This journey has also shaped my mission to empower others. Through my platform, Sip & Heal, I've engaged over 1,800 women in the cities of Atlanta, Dallas, San Diego, Los Angeles, New Orleans, and Charlotte. These gatherings create safe spaces for women to confront and release the shame of past traumas—whether from childhood or adulthood, whether verbal, physical, or emotional. By sharing my story, I aim to help women reclaim their power and recognize their inherent worth.

I can see how much of my identity was shaped by trying to outrun the shame of my past. Perfectionism gave me temporary validation, but it could never fill the void left by trauma. I understand that true worth isn't defined by external success but by embracing who I am, flaws and all. Practicing self-kindness has brought me a peace and fulfillment no accolade ever could. Today, I stand in the truth that I have always been enough—even when I didn't recognize it.

"You find peace

not by rearranging the circumstances of your life,

but by realizing who you are at the deepest level."

— Eckhart Tolle

CHAPTER XXIX

Unlearning Survival, Embracing Peace

> *Peace I leave with you; my peace I give you. I do not give to you as the world gives. Do not let your hearts be troubled and do not be afraid.*
>
> ~ John 14:27 (NIV)

For much of my life, I lived in survival mode, always operating with a plan B, preparing for the worst even when there was no immediate threat. It was a way of life, an ingrained response to the traumas of my past. My default setting was hypervigilance, rooted in an expectation that I would be hurt, let down, or disappointed. Trusting others was a luxury I could not afford. I always had to be one step ahead, always calculating my next move.

The idea of simply existing, of resting in the present without fear or contingency planning, felt foreign and even dangerous. But now, at this stage in my life, I am learning to let go of survival and embrace peace. I no longer need to operate from a place of constant readiness—I am safe now.

Through therapy, I have come to understand that many of the behaviors I thought were personality traits were actually trauma responses. The busyness, the overachievement, the need to control my environment—these were my ways of coping, of ensuring that I never felt powerless again. But in doing so, I exhausted myself, always giving more than I had, always proving my worth through productivity.

I convinced myself that being needed was the same as being valued, and I built my identity around solving other people's problems. What I failed to realize for so long was that peace does not come from constant motion. It comes from within. And now, I am giving myself permission to slow down and simply be.

For years, my schedule was packed beyond reason. I sat on committees, volunteered for causes, took on extra assignments, and was the first to offer help whenever someone was in need. I worked more hours than most of my colleagues, staying tied to my electronic devices at all hours of the day, responding to emails late at night, and checking messages before the sun had even risen.

I wore my busyness as a badge of honor, equating my exhaustion with my importance. I did not know how to exist outside of survival mode, so I buried myself in responsibilities that kept me from confronting the deep exhaustion in my soul. Now, I realize that peace requires space—it cannot flourish in the chaos of overcommitment.

The shift to embracing peace did not happen overnight. It required deep reflection and intentional choices. I had to learn to say no, to prioritize myself, to stop placing my well-being at the bottom of my to-do list. It felt uncomfortable at first, like I was abandoning an old version of myself that had kept me safe. But I remind myself daily that survival mode is not a sustainable way to live—it is a reaction to danger that no longer exists. I am choosing to live fully, not just exist in a state of constant preparedness.

Travel has become one of the greatest gifts of this new chapter in my life. Alvin and I have explored South Africa, Ghana, Greece, London, Spain, Italy, Jamaica, Turks and Caicos, and Mexico, immersing ourselves in different cultures, tasting new foods, and experiencing the beauty of the world. There is something liberating about being somewhere new, with no obligations, no expectations—just the simple joy of discovery.

We have recently expanded our trips to include our children and grandchildren, traveling to Amsterdam, Belgium, Italy, and London together, creating memories that will last a lifetime. These trips remind me that life is about presence, about soaking in moments with the people I love, about allowing joy to be just as much a priority as responsibility once was.

I am ready to breathe. To let go. To enjoy the next several decades focused on my family, speaking to others about my experiences, and walking in my purpose. I no longer feel the need to fill every space with productivity. Some days, I simply sit in stillness, listening to my own thoughts, relishing in the quiet. There is peace in solitude, in knowing that I do not have to prove myself to anyone. I am enough as I am, and that knowledge is freeing.

Embracing peace does not mean my past no longer affects me—it means I no longer let it dictate my present. The wounds are still there, but they are no longer open. They are reminders of what I have overcome, not barriers to my future. I carry them with me, but they do not weigh me down. Instead, they propel me forward, reminding me that healing is a lifelong journey, one that requires patience, self-love, and grace.

I have learned that peace is not something to be chased—it is something to be cultivated. It is in the way I start my mornings, slowly and without urgency. It is in the way I prioritize joy, laughter, and connection over obligation. It is in the moments of deep gratitude, when I look around at my family, and my life, and realize just how far I have come. Survival taught me how to endure, but peace is teaching me how to live.

I no longer need a plan B for everything. I trust myself. I trust that I will handle life's challenges as they come, without living in a constant state of anticipation. I trust the people I have chosen to be in my life, knowing that I am discerning about where I invest my energy. Most importantly, I trust that I deserve this peace, that I am worthy of ease, joy, and contentment.

Letting go of survival mode has been one of the hardest things I have ever done. It is an unraveling, an unlearning, a reprogramming of deeply ingrained beliefs. But with each passing day, it becomes easier. The need to always be busy, to always be bracing for impact, no longer holds power over me. I am finally free.

As I continue this journey, I hope my story encourages others to do the same. To recognize the patterns of survival they have been living in. To question whether their busyness is serving them or exhausting them. To understand that peace is not something given—it is something chosen. And that choice, though difficult, is always worth it. Forgiveness is worth it; faith is the foundation, and healing is the true path to freedom.

I am no longer in survival mode. I am thriving. I am at loved. And for the first time in my life, that is enough.

Acknowledgments

Gratitude fills my heart as I reflect on the incredible people who have stood by me throughout my life. I am blessed with a support system that has shown me love, strength, and unwavering presence through both the beautiful and challenging moments. Their encouragement has shaped my journey, and I am forever thankful.

As an adult, I have gained a deeper understanding of my parents, Ernestine and Arthur Sr. I know without a doubt that they loved all their children. I believe they continue to watch over me, and I pray that my journey—both personally and professionally—makes them proud. Their love, though sometimes imperfect, was always present, and I carry that with me.

I miss my late sisters, Gwen, Joyce, and Mary, deeply. Each of them impacted my life in different ways, providing me with strength, wisdom, and perspective. I tried to share my successes with them over the years as a way of expressing my gratitude for the support they gave me. Though they are no longer physically here, I still feel their love, and I honor their legacy in all that I do.

My brother, Arthur Jr., has become not only our family historian but also a trusted confidant. His words of encouragement and unwavering belief in me have been a source of strength. Our conversations—filled with authenticity and love—have helped me push through some of my most challenging times. His support reminds me that family is not just about shared blood but about shared history, resilience, and love.

I am beyond blessed to have friendships that are more like sisterhoods. Nancy, Annie, Raven, Traci, and Fatou—you are my rocks, my safe space, my tribe. You are the keepers of my secrets, my sources of laughter, and my sanctuary in times of need. There is no doubt in my mind that one call would have you at my doorstep, no questions asked. Thank you for loving me unconditionally, for holding me accountable, and for always giving me grace.

Elder and the late Jackie Nichols stepped in as surrogate parents when I was thousands of miles away from home on the West Coast. Their kindness and guidance were exactly what I needed in that season of my life. Though Jackie is now in heaven, I know she continues to watch over me as one of my angels. I am forever grateful that my work in San Diego led me to them, and I thank God for the impact they made in my life.

To my family—thank you for loving me. My husband, Alvin, and I have spent 30 years growing together, facing life's ups and downs with commitment, forgiveness, and faith. Our marriage has required patience, understanding, and hard work, but the love we have built is strong, and the best is yet to come. I appreciate everything you have been to our family and the foundation we continue to strengthen.

My daughter, Chantell, is my greatest source of pride. She is an extraordinary woman whose kindness, intelligence, and resilience inspire me every day. She has given me the greatest gifts of all—Bryce and Brooklyn. As I continue my journey, I pray that I am a source of encouragement for them, showing them through my life that we are never defined by our past but by the strength we find to move forward.

To my nieces—Pam, Kaminisha, Tamika, Toya, Tasha, Joanna, Alecia, and Jalissa—you are loved as if you were my own daughters. I hope that my path serves as a reminder that no matter what life throws your way, you have the power to overcome, to build, and to thrive. May you continue to chase your dreams, work hard, and forge your own unique trails with confidence and courage.

There are so many more people I can name, so to everyone who has supported me, encouraged me, and stood by me—thank you. Your love, faith, and belief in me have made all the difference. I carry your kindness with me every step of the way.

I will always advocate for the need to reduce the stigma surrounding Black mental health. Mental wellness is not a luxury—it is a necessity. No matter your role in life or the titles you hold, anxiety, depression, and trauma can have a profound impact on your overall well-being. I know this from experience. Through sharing my story, I hope to create space for others to acknowledge their struggles and to seek the support they need and deserve. Healing requires intention, support, and access to services—and it begins with knowing you are not alone.

About the Author

D r. Marie Brown Mercadel is a former public servant who dedicated her career to serving communities nationwide. Born in Jacksonville, North Carolina, she has traveled across the United States supporting her husband, Master Gunnery Sergeant Alvin R. Mercadel, Jr., USMC retired, in his military career.

She completed her undergraduate studies at North Carolina Central University in Durham, North Carolina and her master's and doctorate degree at the University of Phoenix. She is a certified trauma and resilience coach, mentor, presenter, and TEDx speaker who empowers women through her Sip & Heal platform, helping them find their voices and embrace their worth. Her work has been featured on multiple podcasts, in print media, and on local television.

She is a shopping connoisseur and loves to talk about her massive shoe collection. She enjoys cooking, fashion, gardening, traveling, weightlifting, and all things Peloton.

Dr. Brown Mercadel is a proud member of Delta Sigma Theta Sorority, Inc. and is available for book signings and speaking engagements across the country. She resides in the Charlotte, North Carolina area with her husband, Alvin. For more information or to schedule a Sip & Heal event or a keynote speech, please visit her website: https://www.drmariespeaks.com

Photo Gallery

"Never shy away from
using your voice to uplift others.
The courage it takes to share your story
may be the very lifeline someone else needs
to find their own strength,
their own healing, and their own voice."

— Dr. Marie Brown Mercadel

Arthur Brown Sr., (R), Age Unknown

Ernestine Brown,
Age Unknown

The Brown Family

Marie, Fifth Grade

Eisenhower High Graduation Picture, 1982

Marie, 28 and Chantell, 6

Marie, North Carolina Central University graduation

Graduation, University of Phoenix, Master of Arts

Gwen, also known as Nana, my angel

Mary, Joyce, Chantell, and Brooklyn

Marine Corps Ball

Vow renewal, 25 years, the Mercadel family

Marie and Chantell

Elder Howard and Jacqueline Nichols

My brother Arthur Jr. and I

Vow Renewal Ceremony, 25 Years

Alvin and I, Cabo San Lucas

Alvin and I, The Coliseum, Italy

Alvin and I, London, England

Alvin and I, the Acropolis, Greece

Alvin and I, South Africa

Kakum National Park, Accra, Ghana

Black Star Square, Accra, Ghana

Mercadel and Harris-Russell Family, London Eye, Rome, Italy

Bryce, Brooklyn, Alvin, and I at my 60th birthday celebration

The Brown Girls: Brooklyn, Misha, Jalissa, Me, Chantell, and Pam

The Besties: Annie, me, Raven Charlotte

The Besties: Nancy, Raven, Annie, and me, New Orleans

Rock Climbing with Bryce and Brooklyn

My nieces, Toya, Tasha, Joanna, Alexis, And Myasia in New York City

Sip & Heal, Dallas Texas

*Sip & Heal,
Henderson,
North Carolina*

Sip & Heal, Greenville, North Carolina

Sip & Heal, Charlotte, North Carolina

Sip & Heal, San Diego, California

Sip & Heal, Atlanta, Georgia

Sip & Heal, Louisiana

Sip & Heal, Charlotte, North Carolina

*Me and my friend Toroshinia
at Sip & Heal San Diego*

Sip & Heal, Dallas, Texas

Sip & Heal, Louisiana

Book Signing Events

*Speaker, North San Diego County Alumnae
Chapter DST Founders Day Event*

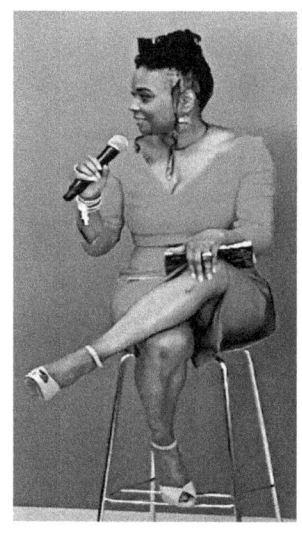

*Speaker, Union County Alumnae
Chapter DST, I'm Every Woman
Conference*

Delta Sigma Theta Sorority, Inc Community Engagement

My Delta Sigma Theta Sorority Line Sorority, Inc
5th year anniversary photo, 8InDSTructible Divas, Aruba
Pictured: Yvette, Taneashia, Glynda, Marie, Carol, Darjené, Vonda

TEDx Talk, Wilmington, Delaware
Photo Credit: Ira Bowman

Living my best life.

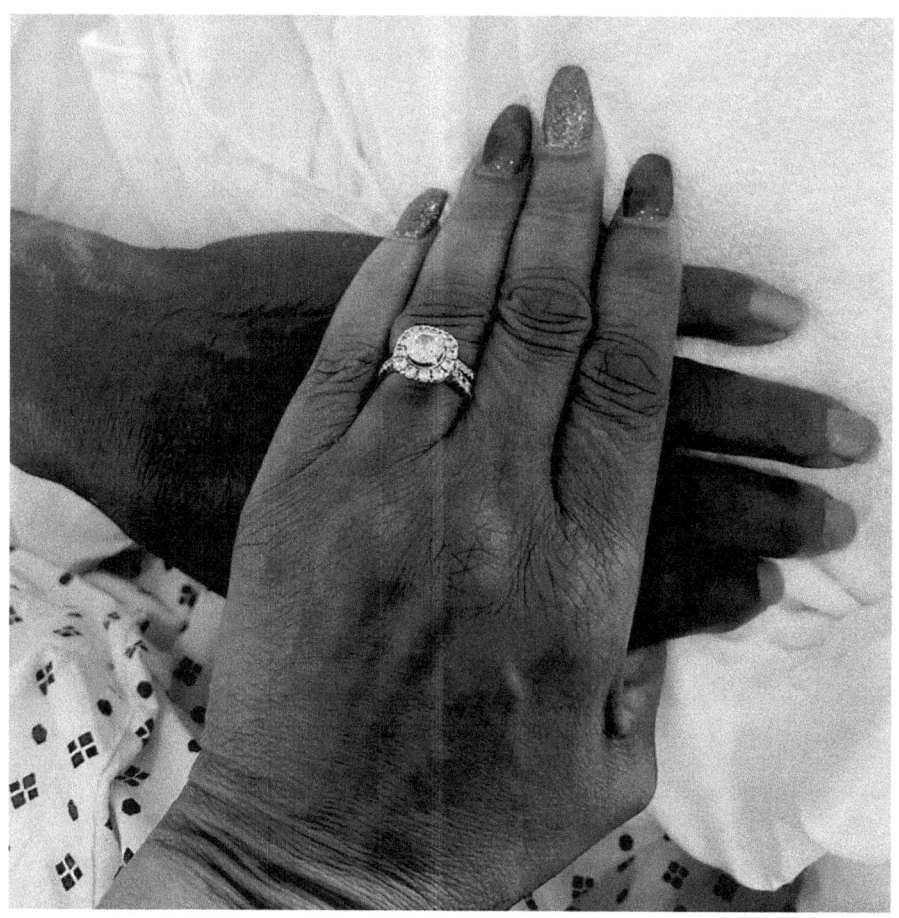

My Brother Edward and I, hand in hand

References

Abrams, J. A., Maxwell, M., Pope, M., & Belgrave, F. Z. (2014). Carrying the world with the grace of a lady and the grit of a warrior: Deepening our understanding of the "Strong Black Woman" schema. *Psychology of Women Quarterly,* 38(4), 503-518.

Bailey, R. K., Patel, M., Barker, N. C., Ali, S., & Jabeen, S. (2017). Racial disparities in access to mental health services among Black and African American individuals. *Journal of Ethnic & Cultural Diversity in Social Work,* 26(2), 121-136.

Beauboeuf-Lafontant, T. (2009). *Behind the mask of the Strong Black Woman: Voice and the embodiment of a costly performance.* Temple University Press.

Bonanno, G. A. (2004). Loss, trauma, and human resilience: Have we underestimated the human capacity to thrive after extremely aversive events? *American Psychologist,* 59(1), 20-28.

Centers for Disease Control and Prevention. (2021). Adverse Childhood Experiences (ACEs). https://www.cdc.gov/violenceprevention/aces/index.html

Enright, R.D., & Fitzgibbons, R.P. (2000). Helping clients forgive: An empirical guide for resolving anger and restoring hope (Washington, DC: *American Psychological Association*), 29.

Felitti, V. J., Anda, R. F., Nordenberg, D., Williamson, D. F., Spitz, A. M., Edwards, V., ... & Marks, J. S. (1998). Relationship of childhood abuse and household dysfunction to many of the leading causes of death in adults: The Adverse Childhood Experiences (ACE) Study. *American Journal of Preventive Medicine,* 14(4), 245-258.

Harris-Perry, M. (2011). *Sister Citizen: Shame, stereotypes, and Black women in America.* Yale University Press.

Henderson, D. X., Lincoln, K. D., & Taylor, R. J. (2021). The impact of racial trauma on mental health in Black communities. *American Journal of Community Psychology,* 67(1-2), 42-56.

Herman, J. L. (1997). *Trauma and recovery: The aftermath of violence—from domestic abuse to political terror.* Basic Books.

Joseph, S., & Linley, P. A. (2005). Positive psychological perspectives on posttraumatic stress: An integrative review. *Clinical Psychology Review,* 26(8), 1041-1053.

Masten, A. S., & Barnes, A. J. (2018). *Resilience in children: Developmental perspectives.* Children, 5(7), 98.

McCullough, M. E., Pargament, K. I., & Thoresen, C. E. (2000). *Forgiveness: Theory, research, and practice.* Guilford Press.

Neff, K. D. (2011). Self-compassion, self-esteem, and well-being. *Social and Personality Psychology Compass,* 5(1), 1-12.

Neff, K. D., & Germer, C. K. (2013). A pilot study and randomized controlled trial of the mindful self-compassion program. *Journal of Clinical Psychology, 69*(1), 28-44.

Pargament, K. I. (2001). *The psychology of religion and coping: Theory, research, and practice.* Guilford Press.

Pennebaker, J. W. (1997). *Opening up: The healing power of expressing emotions.* Guilford Press.

Shonkoff, J. P., Garner, A. S., Siegel, B. S., Dobbins, M. I., Earls, M. F., McGuinn, L., & Pascoe, J. (2012). The lifelong effects of early childhood adversity and toxic stress. *Pediatrics,* 129(1), e232-e246.

Tedeschi, R. G., & Calhoun, L. G. (2004). Posttraumatic growth: Conceptual foundations and empirical evidence. *Psychological Inquiry,* 15(1), 1-18.

Turney, K., & Haskins, A. R. (2014). Falling behind? Children's early grade retention after paternal incarceration. *Sociology of Education,* 87(4), 241-258.

van der Kolk, B. (2014). *The body keeps the score: Brain, mind, and body in the healing of trauma.* Viking.

Williams, M. T., Metzger, I. W., Leins, C., & DeLapp, R. C. (2020). Reducing mental health disparities through culturally adapted interventions for Black individuals. *Clinical Psychology: Science and Practice,* 27(3), e12324.

Woods-Giscombe, C. L. (2010). Superwoman schema: African American women's views on stress, strength, and health. *Qualitative Health Research,* 20(5), 668-683.

Worthington, E. L., & Scherer, M. (2004). Forgiveness is an emotion-focused coping strategy that can reduce health risks and promote health resilience: Theory, review, and hypotheses. *Psychology & Health, 19*(3), 385-405.

Yates, P. (2021). Sibling sexual abuse: A knowledge and practice overview. Center of Expertise on Child Sexual Abuse. Csacentre.org.uk

Yehuda, R., & Lehrner, A. (2018). Intergenerational transmission of trauma effects: putative role of epigenetic mechanisms. *World Psychiatry*, 17(3), 243-257.

Resources

American Psychological Association: A professional organization that promotes the health and well-being of members of society by conducting research that addresses substance abuse, violence, and mental and physical health. www.apa.org

Black Emotional and Mental Health Collective. An institution that is dedicated to the wellbeing, healing, and liberation of black and marginalized communities. The mission is to remove the barriers faced by the Black community by providing education, training, advocacy, and education. Beam.community

Black Mental Health Alliance. The Alliance promotes trusted culturally relevant educational forums, training, and referral services that support the health and well-being of Black people and their communities. Blackmentalhealth.com

Black Therapist Rock: A network of Black therapists that provides culturally relevant mental health services that address the lifelong impacts of racial trauma and strives to reduce the sigma related to mental health. Blacktherapistrock.com

Cerebral: Expert help to manage anxiety, depression, and other mental health disorders. The services provided include evaluation and assessment, medication management, and telephone or video sessions with a licensed therapist. Cerebral.com

Center for Young Women's Health: The Center is an educational entity that exists to provide adolescents of all genders with carefully researched health information, health education programs, and community spaces. Youngwomenshealth.org

MeToo movement: A social movement supporting the goal of eradicating sexual abuse and sexual harassment. Resources are available for survivors to learn how to heal and develop a sense of safety. www.Metoomvmt.org

National Alliance on Mental Illness: A grassroots behavioral health organization that is committed to improving the lives of the millions of people that are affected by mental illness. Nami.org

National Suicide Prevention Lifeline: A national network of local crisis centers that provides free and confidential supports to people that are experiencing a suicidal crisis. Suicideprevention.org

Psychology Today Directory of African American Therapists. Provides a detailed listing of Black therapists across the United States. psychologytoday.com

RAINN National Sexual Assault Telephone Hotline: RAINN partners with a network of service providers nationally to prevent sexual violence and offer resources for victims and survivors. Rain.org

Substance Abuse and Mental Health Services Administration. This organization offers a national hotline that is available 24/7 365-days-a-year to individuals and families who are facing mental and/or substance abuse disorders. samhsa.gov

Society for Adolescent Health and Medicine (SAHM). This site provides mental health resources for adolescents and young adults information about support groups, peer networks, helplines, treatment locators, and advocacy opportunities. adolescenthealth.org

The Kennedy Forum. The organization focuses on coverage parity and is dedicated to ensuring that individuals have access to treatment for mental health and substance abuse disorders. thekennedyforum.org

Therapy for Black Girls. An online space dedicated to encouraging the mental wellness of Black women and girls. Therapyforblackgirls.com

Therapy For Black Men: A community mental health resource that focuses on breaking the stigma associated with receiving mental health services. This therapeutic resource provides a directory of Black service providers and information about services for Black men. Therapyforblackmen.org

Winoverdepression.org : A podcast, YouTube Channel, and website created by a survivor who has suffered from depression for most of her adult life. The Podcast provides information about services, resources, and coping strategies

Adverse Childhood Experiences Survey

(reprinted with permission from the CDC public domain)

The Adverse Childhood Experiences Study was conducted by the Centers for Disease Control and Prevention and Kaiser Permanente. The study included seventeen thousand adults and was initiated for the purpose of examining the lifelong impact of traumatic events experienced by children. The data for the survey may be accessed at: cdc.gov/violenceprevention/aces.

The survey questions are listed below:

While you were growing up, during your first eighteen years of life:

1. Did a parent or other adult in the household often: swear at you, insult you, put you down, or humiliate you?

OR

   Act in a way that made you afraid that you might be physically hur?t

   ☐ Yes ☐ No   If Yes, enter 1 _____

2. Did a parent or other adult in the household often: push, grab, slap, or throw something at you?

   OR

   Ever hit you so hard that you had marks or were injured?

   ☐ Yes ☐ No If Yes, enter 1 _____

3. Did an adult or a person at least five years older than you ever: Touch or fondle you or have you touch their body in a sexual way?

   OR

   Attempt or have oral, anal, or vaginal intercourse with you?

   ☐ Yes ☐ No If Yes, enter 1 _____

4 Did you often feel that: No one in your family loved you or thought that you were important or special?

   OR

   Your family didn't look out for each other, feel close to each other, or support each other?

   ☐ Yes ☐ No If Yes, enter 1 _____

5. Did you often feel that: You didn't have enough to eat, had to wear dirty clothes, and had no one to protect you?

   OR

   Your parents were too drunk or high to take care of you or take you to the doctor if you needed it?

   ☐ Yes ☐ No If Yes, enter 1 _____

6. Were your parents ever separated or divorced?

   ☐ Yes ☐ No If Yes, enter 1 _____

7. Were any of your parents or other adult caregivers often pushed, grabbed, slapped, or had something thrown at them?

   OR

   Sometimes or often kicked, bitten, hit with a fist, or hit with something?

   Ever repeatedly hit over at least a few minutes or threatened with a gun or knife?

   ☐ Yes ☐ No If Yes, enter 1 _____

8. Did you live with anyone who was a problem drinker or alcoholic or who used street drugs?

   ☐ Yes ☐ No If Yes, enter 1 _____

9. Was a household member depressed or mentally ill, or did a household member attempt suicide?

   ☐ Yes ☐ No If Yes, enter 1 _____

10. Did a household member go to prison?

    ☐ Yes ☐ No If Yes, enter 1 _____

ACE SCORE (Total Yes Answers): _____

ACES QR Code (Scan to Complete) **
Adverse Childhood Experiences Survey

** The data will be captured and aggregated in a database for future research, the survey responses are anonymous.

www.ingramcontent.com/pod-product-compliance
Lightning Source LLC
Chambersburg PA
CBHW071729120626
46550CB00002B/447